2018

FIELD GUIDE TO

CLASSIC FARM TRACTORS

FIELD GUIDE TO

CLASSIC
FARM
TRACTORS

TEXT BY
Robert N. Pripps

PHOTOGRAPHS BY
Ralph W. Sanders, Andrew Morland,
and Gary A. Nelson

Voyageur
Press

Quarto is the authority on a wide range of topics.

Quarto educates, entertains and enriches the lives of our readers—enthusiasts and lovers of hands-on living.

www.quartoknows.com

First published in 2016 by Voyageur Press, an imprint of Quarto Publishing Group USA Inc., 400 First Avenue North, Suite 400, Minneapolis, MN 55401 USA. Telephone: (612) 344-8100 Fax: (612) 344-8692

quartoknows.com
Visit our blogs at quartoknows.com

Voyageur Press titles are also available at discounts in bulk quantity for industrial or sales-promotional use. For details contact the Special Sales Manager at Quarto Publishing Group USA Inc., 400 First Avenue North, Suite 400, Minneapolis, MN 55401 USA.

10 9 8 7 6 5 4 3 2 1

ISBN: 978-0-7603-5012-6

Library of Congress Cataloging-in-Publication Data

Names: Pripps, Robert N., 1932- author.
Title: Field guide to classic farm tractors / text by Robert N. Pripps ;
   photographs by Ralph W. Sanders, Andrew Morland, and Gary A. Nelson.
Description: Minneapolis, MN, USA : Voyageur Press, 2016. | Includes
   bibliographical references and index.
Identifiers: LCCN 2016006710 | ISBN 9780760350126 (paperback)
Subjects: LCSH: Farm tractors--Collectors and collecting. | Farm
   tractors--History. | Antique and classic tractors--Pictorial works. |
   BISAC: ANTIQUES & COLLECTIBLES / Transportation. | ANTIQUES &
COLLECTIBLES
   / Americana.
Classification: LCC TL233.6.F37 P7494 2016 | DDC 631.3/72--dc23
LC record available at http://lccn.loc.gov/2016006710

Acquiring Editor: Todd R. Berger
Project Manager: Caitlin Fultz
Art Director: James Kegley
Layout: Amy Sly

On the front cover: *Ralph W. Sanders*
On the back cover (all): *Ralph W. Sanders*

Printed in China

CONTENTS

Introduction

This book is intended to provide thumbnail sketches of popular classic farm tractors, both domestic and foreign. Hopefully we've covered the one you're looking for and provided the information you need, whether you are attending a tractor show or auction or answering a "for sale" advertisement. Pictures were mostly provided by the photographers Ralph W. Sanders, Andrew Morland, and Gary A. Nelson, although a few have been provided by the author.

Technical data has been taken from the University of Nebraska's Tractor Test Laboratory (NTTL) reports. The Nebraska Tractor Test Act, passed in July 1919, requires all tractors sold in the state to pass tests conducted by the University of Nebraska. The results of these tests have become the recognized standard for tractor comparisons. Test numbers are provided beneath specifications tables for specific models. In some cases, where the tractor did not undergo such testing, the manufacturer's data was used.

Just a few notes before getting started: Kerosene was a popular fuel into the 1940s. Improved kerosene was called distillate or tractor fuel. Rather than list the number of transmission ratios, we have used an abbreviated form. For instance, 4f-2r means four forward speeds and two reverse speeds.

The "unit frame" concept refers to the practice of employing the engine, transmission, and rear axle castings as the tractor's frame, rather than the conventional channel-iron frame.

Several common abbreviations are defined as follows:

LPG = liquefied petroleum gas, or propane

PTO = power take-off, or the power output other than to the drive wheels

FWA = front-wheel assist, a form of front-wheel drive, usually by means of hydraulic motors in the front-wheel assemblies

Dedicated classic tractor enthusiasts restored and displayed the photographed tractors. They not only spent time and money bringing these treasures to sometimes better-than-new conditions, but they also took the time to get them out, dust them off, and move them around for us to get these photos. Thank you!

The Big Boys

Allis-Chalmers

Milwaukee, Wisconsin

In 1901, Allis-Chalmers was formed through a merger of E. P. Allis & Co. and several other companies, including one owned in part by William J. Chalmers of Chicago. The firm produced flour-milling equipment, sawmill gear, electrical paraphernalia, and steam engines. Hard times hit Allis-Chalmers in 1912, and it went into receivership. It was at that time that Otto H. Falk, as receiver, began his twenty years at the helm of the company, on which he left a lasting mark.

General Falk (he was a general in the Wisconsin National Guard) soon recognized that all of his eggs were in the heavy-manufacturing industry, with little real diversity. This led to several tractor designs, but success in the farm-equipment business required a dealer network and branch houses. It was not until 1931, with the acquisition of the Advance-Rumely Thresher Company, that things really took off. The company became known for its bright orange livery, thanks to Harry Merritt, manager of the tractor division—which pioneered such industry advancements as standard rubber tires, power-adjustable rear rims, and turbochargers.

Allis-Chalmers was involved in various kinds of energy research in the 1960s, including nuclear power, but agricultural expansion to overseas markets proved unsuccessful. In 1985, German KHD (Klöckner-Humboldt-Deutz) acquired the Allis-Chalmers agricultural businesses, forming Deutz-Allis. In 1990, these assets were acquired in a management buyout and renamed AGCO (Allis-Gleaner Corporation), which continues to the present time.

ALLIS-CHALMERS
10-18 AND 6-12

The 10-18 was the first Allis-Chalmers tractor. It had a three-wheel design quite similar to the Massey-Harris Bull Tractor (see page 113) and the Happy Farmer of Minneapolis's Happy Farmer Tractor Company. Like the others, the 10-18 had its single front wheel in line with the right rear, allowing it to "self-guide" by running in the previous plow furrow. The concept did not prove to be popular with farmers, and fewer than three thousand are estimated to have been built. The 10-18 boasted a rigid one-piece steel frame.

BELOW 1914 Allis-Chalmers 10-18

PREVIOUS SPREAD 1952 Allis-Chalmers WD

SPECIFICATIONS

10-18

Engine: 2-cylinder, horizontally opposed

Bore and stroke: 5.25×7.00 in.

Displacement: 303 ci., kerosene fuel

Power: 10 drawbar hp, 18 belt hp; 1-plow rating

Transmission: 1f-1r

Top speed: 2.3 mph

Weight: 4,800 lb.

1919 Allis-Chalmers 6-12

The Allis-Chalmers 6-12 was of a very different design from that of the 10-18 and resembled, instead, the Moline Universal (see page 131). The tractor had only two wheels and relied on a sulky, a wheeled implement, to carry the back end. Development began in 1915, but production did not start until after the end of World War I, in 1919. Ongoing protests by the Moline Plow Company regarding patent infringement accounted for some of the delay. It is believed that Allis-Chalmers ended up paying royalties to Moline. A LeRoi engine was used.

6-12

Engine: 4-cylinder LeRoi, vertical, side valve

Bore and stroke: 3.125×4.500 in.

Displacement: 138 ci., kerosene fuel

Power: 6 drawbar hp, 12 belt hp; 1-plow rating

Transmission: 1f-1r

Top speed: 2.5 mph

Weight: 2,500 lb.

VARIATIONS

10-18 (1914–1921), 6-12 (1919–1926)

1930 Allis-Chalmers U

ALLIS-CHALMERS
U AND UC

The U was initially designed for the United Tractor and Equipment Corporation and manufactured for them by Allis-Chalmers. United soon disappeared, and in 1929, Allis-Chalmers offered the tractor to its dealers as the Allis-Chalmers United. The following year, the designation was changed to the U. The first 7,404 tractors used a Continental side-valve four-cylinder engine. Subsequent units were equipped with Allis-Chalmers's own overhead-valve four. The U and UC were the first tractors to be painted in the A-C trademark Persian Orange.

The U had the distinction of being the first farm tractor to be offered for sale with low-pressure pneumatic tires as an option. (Steel wheels were still standard equipment.) Its row crop running mate, the UC, was equipped with a power lift for its drive-in cultivator.

SPECIFICATIONS

U

Engine: 4-cylinder Allis-Chalmers, overhead valve

Bore and stroke: 4.375×5.000 in.

Displacement: 300 ci., distillate fuel

Power: 22 drawbar hp, 33 belt hp; 3-plow rating

Transmission: 4f-1r

Top speed: 10 mph

Weight: 5,100 lb.

NTTL# 237

VARIATIONS

United (1929), U and UC with Continental engine (1930–1932), U with Allis-Chalmers engine (1933–1944), UC with Allis-Chalmers engine (1933–1941)

1931 Allis-Chalmers UC

ALLIS-CHALMERS
WC AND WD

The WC was introduced in late 1933, with mild styling and a radiator grille. The 1938 version featured full styling, retained into the late 1950s. The WC was the first farm tractor to be offered with rubber tires as standard equipment; steel wheels were still an option. The drive-wheel tires were the first tires to be filled three-quarters of the way with a freeze-resistant liquid for added weight and traction, known as Hydromatics. The WC used a steel channel frame. There were both kerosene and gasoline engine versions. The standard-tread running mate to the WC was the WF, introduced in 1940 and produced through 1951.

The WD succeeded the WC in 1948. The WD boasted the first power-adjustable rear-wheel tread. It was also available with hydraulics and a semi-live power take-off, or PTO. (As long as the main clutch was engaged, the PTO was independent of ground speed.) The same engine was used, but its rated speed was increased to 1,400 rpm. The WD was available in dual-tricycle, single, and adjustable wide front ends.

SPECIFICATIONS
WC and WF

Engine: 4-cylinder Allis-Chalmers, overhead valve

Bore and stroke: 4.00×4.00 in.

Displacement: 201 ci., kerosene (distillate) fuel

Power: 12 drawbar hp, 22 belt hp; 2-plow rating

Transmission: 4f-1r

Top speed: 9 mph

Weight: 3,200 lb.

WD-45

Engine: 4-cylinder Allis-Chalmers, overhead valve

Bore and stroke: 4.00×4.50 in.

Displacement: 226 ci., gasoline fuel

Power: 30 drawbar hp, 40 belt hp; 3-plow rating

Transmission: 4f-1r

Top speed: 11 mph

Weight: 4,000 lb.

NTTL# 499

1933 Allis-Chalmers WC

1955 Allis-Chalmers WD-45

The WD was followed in 1953 by the WD-45, built along the same lines. A significant new feature was power steering—soon to be copied by all other tractor manufacturers. The WD-45 engine retained the 4.00 bore, but the stroke was increased to 4.50 inches, giving it substantially more power. It could be ordered configured for gasoline, dual-fuel (kerosene or gasoline), or LPG (liquefied petroleum gas) versions. In 1956, the WD-45D six-cylinder diesel was offered.

WD-45D

Engine: 6-cylinder Allis-Chalmers, overhead valve

Bore and stroke: 3.38×4.13 in.

Displacement: 230 ci., diesel fuel

Power: 30 drawbar hp, 43 belt hp; 3-plow rating

Transmission: 4f-1r

Top speed: 12 mph

Weight: 4,300 lb.

NTTL# 563

VARIATIONS

WC (1933–1948), WF (1940–1951), WD (1948–1953), WD-45 (1953–1957), WD-45D diesel (1955–1957)

1948 Allis-Chalmers G

ALLIS-CHALMERS
G

The Allis-Chalmers G, announced in 1948 as a "hoe on wheels," was unique among farm tractors of its time. It featured a rear-mounted 10-horsepower Continental four-cylinder engine, with the operator's seat ahead of the engine. Tubular frame members extended forward, locating the front wheels and providing a mounting place for various implements designed to appeal to truck gardeners, nurserymen, and highway mowers. Visibility, especially for guiding the cultivator, was unimpeded. The steering wheel even had a segment of the rim omitted, to avoid blocking the view. The four-speed transmission was provided with a special "low" first gear for cultivating delicate plants at less than 1 mile per hour. The tiny four-cylinder engine was virtually the same as that used in the Farmall Cub and Massey-Harris Pony.

SPECIFICATIONS

G

Engine: 4-cylinder Continental, side valve

Bore and stroke: 2.375×3.500 in.

Displacement: 62 ci., gasoline fuel

Power: 7 drawbar hp, 10 belt hp; 1-plow rating

Transmission: 4f-1r

Top speed: 7 mph

Weight: 1,550 lb.

NTTL# 398

VARIATIONS

G (1948–1955)

ALLIS-CHALMERS
B, C, AND CA

The "Allis B" (B) was a small general-purpose row crop machine aimed at replacing a team of horses. The B featured wide-set front wheels with an arched front axle. The rear tread was adjustable in tread width. The BI ("industrial") was the same tractor but modified for industrial use, with a straight front axle and smaller, nonadjustable rear wheels. It was equipped with a foot brake and foot-feed throttle.

For 1939, the B was upgraded to the C, which had a tricycle front end and a more powerful engine and was equipped with a wide bench seat. Hydraulics became an option on the C. In 1949, Allis came out with the CA. Power was boosted by raising the engine speed. The CA had the option of either tricycle or adjustable wide front ends. It featured a hydraulic implement lift with the new "Snap-Coupler" implement hitch and a new four-speed transmission, but it reverted to a pan seat. It also had individual foot brakes, as did later Cs.

SPECIFICATIONS

B and BI

Engine: 4-cylinder Allis-Chalmers, overhead valve

Bore and stroke: 3.25×3.50 in.

Displacement: 116 ci., distillate fuel

Power: 10 drawbar hp, 15 hp belt; 1-plow rating

Transmission: 3f-1r

Top speed: 8 mph

Weight: 2,130 lb.

NTTL# 302

C

Engine: 4-cylinder Allis-Chalmers, overhead valve

Bore and stroke: 3.375×3.500 in.

Displacement: 125 ci., distillate fuel

Power: 13 drawbar hp, 19 belt hp; 2-plow rating

Transmission: 3f-1r

Top speed: 8 mph

Weight: 2,400 lb.

NTTL# 363

1941 Allis-Chalmers C

ABOVE 1951 Allis-Chalmers CA

TOP 1938 Allis-Chalmers B

CA

Engine: 4-cylinder Allis-Chalmers, overhead valve

Bore and stroke: 3.375×3.500 in.

Displacement: 125 ci., gasoline fuel

Power: 18 drawbar hp, 25 belt hp; 2-plow rating

Transmission: 4f-1r

Top speed: 11 mph

Weight: 2,700 lb.

NTTL# 453

VARIATIONS

B (1938–1957), BI (1939–1957), C (1940–1948), CA (1949–1957)

Allis-Chalmers D-14

ALLIS-CHALMERS
D-14 AND D-15

Introduced in 1958, the D-14 signaled the transition to a completely new line of A-C tractors. Low-compression fuel options were no longer available, and for gasoline, the compression ratio was 7.5:1. With LPG fuel, it rose to 8.5:1. Built-in power steering was an option, as was the new Power-Director partial-range power shift. Also new was the Roll-Shift wide front axle, which allowed the front-wheel tread to be changed by driving the tractor forward or backward. Rice and orchard specials were offered, as was the standard configuration with tricycle or wide front ends.

SPECIFICATIONS
D-14

Engine: 4-cylinder Allis-Chalmers, overhead valve

Bore and stroke: 3.250×3.875 in.

Displacement: 149 ci., gasoline fuel

Power: 33 drawbar, 25 belt hp; 3-plow rating

Transmission: 8f-2r with partial-range shift

Top speed: 12 mph

Weight: 3,700 lb.

NTTL# 623

The D-14 was superseded by the D-15 in 1960. It used the same 149-cubic-inch engine for gasoline and LPG, but the rated rpm was raised from 1,650 to 2,000. A 175-cubic-inch diesel was added to the line. A category 1 three-point hitch was an option, as were grove (orchard) and industrial versions. A D-15 Series II came out in 1962 with a more powerful gasoline engine. The diesel version had a heavy-duty clutch, which became an option on the Series II gasoline version. The Roll-Shift wide front, standard wide front, tricycle, and single-front-wheel front ends were also options on the D-15.

D-15 Series II

Engine: 4-cylinder Allis-Chalmers, overhead valve

Bore and stroke: 3.63×3.88 in.

Displacement: 160 ci., gasoline fuel

Power: 38 drawbar hp, 46 belt hp; 3-plow rating

Transmission: 8f-2r with partial-range shift

Top speed: 15 mph

Weight: 4,025 lb.

NTTL# 837

VARIATIONS

D-14 (1958–1959), D-15 (1960–1968)

1966 Allis-Chalmers D-15 Series II

ALLIS-CHALMERS
D-17

The Allis-Chalmers D-17 was available in four-cylinder LPG and gasoline engines or a six-cylinder diesel. Features included the Roll-Shift front axle system, power steering, and the eight-speed Power-Director power shift transmission. The D-17 was produced in four series, with trim and decals being the only differences (with the exception of the Series IV being available with a three-point hitch). D-17 came with single and dual-tricycle fronts as well as an adjustable wide front end. Wheatland and orchard fenders were options, as was a utility version for use with end loaders, backhoes, and industrial applications.

1958 Allis-Chalmers D-17

SPECIFICATIONS

D-17 (Gasoline)

Engine: 4-cylinder Allis-Chalmers, overhead valve

Bore and stroke: 4.00×4.50 in.

Displacement: 226 ci., gasoline fuel

Power: 37 drawbar hp, 50 hp belt; 3-plow rating

Transmission: 8f-2r with partial-range shift

Top speed: 12 mph

Weight: 4,700 lb.

NTTL# 635

D-17 (Diesel)

Engine: 6-cylinder Allis-Chalmers, overhead valve

Bore and stroke: 3.563×4.375 in.

Displacement: 262 ci., diesel fuel

Power: 36 drawbar hp, 51 belt hp; 3-plow rating

Transmission: 8f-2r

Top speed: 12mph

Weight: 4,900 lb.

NTTL# 636

VARIATIONS

D-17 (1957–1959), Series II (1959–1964), Series III (1964–1965), Series IV (1965–1967)

ALLIS-CHALMERS
D-19

Allis-Chalmers's D-19 diesel was the first production tractor to use a turbocharger. The model was also available with LPG and gasoline engines; only the diesel incorporated the turbocharger. Allis-Chalmers was one of the largest producers of turbochargers for aircraft in World War II. All engines were six-cylinder types of 262 cubic inches. Tricycle and Roll-Shift wide fronts were options, as was a high-clearance model. Either a category 2 three-point hitch or the A-C Snap-Coupler hitch could be ordered.

1963 Allis-Chalmers D-19

D-19 (Gasoline)

Engine: 6-cylinder Allis-Chalmers, overhead valve

Bore and stroke: 3.56×4.38 in.

Displacement: 262 ci., gasoline fuel

Power: 64 drawbar hp, 72 belt hp; 5-plow rating

Transmission: 8f-2r with partial-range shift

Top speed: 14 mph

Weight: 6,800 lb.

NTTL# 810

D-19 (Diesel)

Engine: 6-cylinder Allis-Chalmers, overhead valve, turbocharged

Bore and stroke: 3.56×4.38 in.

Displacement: 262 ci., diesel fuel

Power: 62 drawbar hp, 67 hp belt; 5-plow rating

Transmission: 8f-2r with partial-range shift

Top speed: 14 mph

Weight: 6,800 lb.

NTTL# 811

VARIATIONS

D-19 (1961–1963)

ALLIS-CHALMERS
D-10 AND D-12

The Allis-Chalmers D-10 and D-12 were the same, except for wheel-tread width. The D-10's tread was narrower and designed for one-row cultivation; that of the D-12 was wider, for two-row cultivation. Both models were available in high-clearance versions. Engine displacement was increased at serial number 3,501. Gasoline was the only fuel option. Trim differences were noted between Series I and Series II. For Series III, a 12-volt electrical system, adjustable front axles (on the D-12), and hydraulics were added. The headlights were also moved from the radiator grille to the rear fenders for Series III, to accommodate front-end loaders.

1963 Allis-Chalmers D-12 Series II

SPECIFICATIONS
D-10 and D-12

Engine: 4-cylinder Allis-Chalmers, overhead valve

Bore and stroke: 3.38×3.88 in.

Displacement: 139 ci., gasoline fuel

Power: 26 drawbar hp, 29 belt hp; 2-plow rating

Transmission: 4f-1r

Top speed: 11 mph

Weight: 2,860 lb.

NTTL# 724

After S/N 3,501

Engine: 4-cylinder Allis-Chalmers, overhead valve

Bore and stroke: 3.50×3.88 in.

Displacement: 149 ci., gasoline fuel

Power: 29 drawbar hp, 33 belt hp; 2-plow rating

Transmission: 4f-1r

Top speed: 11 mph

Weight: 3,051 lb.

NTTL# 813

VARIATIONS

D-10–D-12 (1959–1961), Series II (1962–1963), Series III (1964–1967)

ALLIS-CHALMERS
D-21

A six-cylinder diesel engine, naturally aspirated and featuring direct fuel injection, powered the Allis-Chalmers D-21. The D-21 was produced in agricultural and industrial versions, but the main difference between the two was the paint color: Persian Range for the ag model and Highway Yellow for the industrial. A Series II version used the same engine, equipped with a turbocharger. Both Series I and II used an eight-speed fixed ratio transmission. Power steering was standard, as was a category 3 three-point hitch with lower-link draft control.

1968 Allis-Chalmers D-21 Series II

SPECIFICATIONS

D-21 Series I

Engine: 6-cylinder Allis-Chalmers, overhead valve

Bore and stroke: 4.50×5.00 in.

Displacement: 426 ci., diesel fuel

Power: 93 drawbar hp, 103 hp belt; 8-plow rating

Transmission: 8f-2r

Top speed: 16 mph

Weight: 10,745 lb.

NTTL# 855

D-21 Series II

Engine: 6-cylinder Allis-Chalmers, overhead valve, turbocharged

Bore and stroke: 4.50×5.00 in.

Displacement: 426 ci., diesel fuel

Power: 116 drawbar hp, 127 PTO hp; 10-plow rating

Transmission: 8f-2r

Top speed: 16 mph

Weight: 10,675 lb.

NTTL# 904

VARIATIONS

D-21 (1963–1964), Series II (1965–1969)

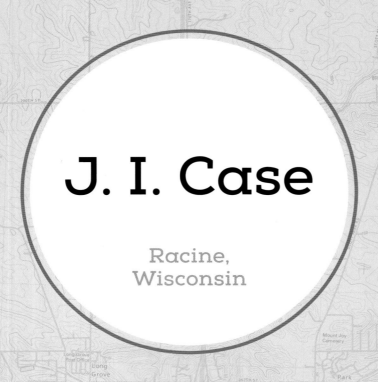

J. I. Case

Racine, Wisconsin

In 1843, twenty-two-year-old Jerome Increase Case set up shop in Rochester, Wisconsin Territory, and began tinkering with machines to thresh grain. Case was one of several inventive geniuses in agriculture at that time who had a profound effect not only on farming, but on society in general: John Deere, Cyrus McCormick, Daniel Massey, Alanson Harris, and James Oliver. These pioneers revolutionized agriculture, prodded the Industrial Revolution into existence, and changed the way people lived.

Case selected Rochester because the town was named after his boyhood hometown of Rochester, New York. Unfortunately for Rochester, the city's fathers would not grant Case the rights to the industrial water-power system, so he moved his threshing-machine manufacturing operation downriver to the shores of Lake Michigan, to the small town of Racine. Within five years, Case was the largest employer in the newly formed state of Wisconsin.

Case became well known for steam engines, but they made their first attempt at an internal combustion tractor in 1892. Carburetion and ignition difficulties forced the further development of internal combustion tractors to be postponed until 1910.

The J. I. Case Company, which absorbed many important competitors over the years (including International Harvester), is still headquartered on the banks of Lake Michigan in Racine, Wisconsin. It is now part of one of the largest agricultural equipment manufacturers in the world, having been folded into the gigantic Fiat family of companies.

CASE
30-60 AND 20-40

The first in this series of two-cylinder Case tractors was the 30-60. It had a four-cycle cross-mounted engine with horizontal and side-by-side cylinders. Pistons moved in unison for even firing. The 30-60's riveted frame had 10-inch channels. It was equipped with a two-speed transmission and foot-operated brake. Cooling was done by exhaust-induced draft. Drive wheels were 6 feet in diameter, with 12-inch faces.

Following in short order, with the same general configuration, was the 20-40. The 20-40 used a two-cylinder horizontally opposed engine, increased in displacement in 1916 from 904 cubic inches to 1,082 cubic inches without changing the rating. Also in 1916, the cooling tower radiator was changed to the now-conventional radiator and fan. Unlike its competitors, Case used water as the cooling medium, rather than oil.

1913 Case 30-60

SPECIFICATIONS

30-60

Engine: 2-cylinder, horizontal, side-by-side, overhead valve

Bore and stroke: 5.25×7.00 in.

Displacement: 1,885 ci., kerosene fuel

Power: 30 drawbar hp, 60 belt hp; 8-plow rating

Transmission: 2f-1r

Top speed: 2 mph

Weight: 26,000 lb.

20-40

Engine: 2-cylinder, horizontally opposed, overhead valve

Bore and stroke: 8.75×9.00 in.

Displacement: 1,082 ci. (final), kerosene fuel

Power: 25 drawbar hp, 40 belt hp; 6-plow rating

Transmission: 2f-1r

Top speed: 3 mph

Weight: 13,780 lb.

NTTL# 7

VARIATIONS

30-60 (1912–1916), 20-40 (1912–1919)

CASE
CROSSMOTOR
9-18 AND 10-18

Adapting the four-cylinder vertical engine from the Case automobile, mounted crosswise, to a new line of tractors, Case arrived at the Crossmotor series. The first of these was the 9-18, which came out in 1916. The 9-18B followed in 1918 and was essentially the same, except that the channel-iron frame was replaced with a cast-iron frame. A further modification, the 10-18 also debuted in 1918. It was the same as the 9-18B, other than a heavier crankshaft, governed speed that increased to 1,050 rpm from 900, water pump cooling, and a pressure lubrication system.

SPECIFICATIONS

Crossmotor 9-18

Engine: 4-cylinder Case, vertical, transverse, overhead valve

Bore and stroke: 3.88×5.00 in.

Displacement: 236 ci., kerosene fuel

Power: 9 drawbar hp, 18 belt hp; 2-plow rating

Transmission: 2f-1r

Top speed: 3 mph

Weight: 3,700 lb.

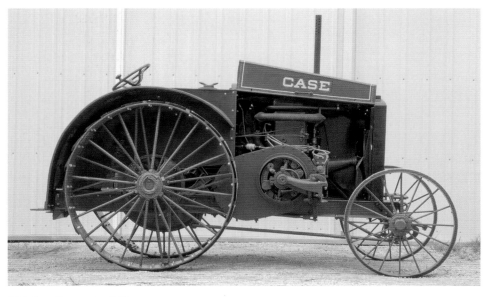

1916 Case Crossmotor 9-18

1919 Case Crossmotor 10-18

This series of tractors had hoods and side panels covering the engine, with a radiator in front. The fully enclosed transmission and drivetrain led to the differential in the left rear-wheel hub. A hand-operated clutch was mounted on an arm extending to the right side of the tractor. The series featured the new Case "water washer" air cleaner.

Crossmotor 10-18

Engine: 4-cylinder Case, vertical, transverse, overhead valve

Bore and stroke: 3.88×5.00 in.

Displacement: 236 ci.

Power: 11 drawbar hp, 18 belt hp; 3-plow rating

Transmission: 2f-1r

Top speed: 4 mph

Weight: 3,760 lb.

NTTL# 3

VARIATIONS

9-18 (1916–1918), 9-18B (1918–1918), 10-18 (1918–1922)

CASE
CROSSMOTOR 15-27, 12-20, AND 40-72

Case's 15-27, introduced in 1919, was fourth in the Crossmotor series. It was similar to the 10-18, which continued in parallel until 1922. The 15-27, which also went by the designations 18-32 and K, had its rated engine speed increased from 900 to 1,000 rpm. Both differed in appearance from the 10-18 mainly in that the exhaust pipe was bent to the left to keep gasses away from the operator. Case continued to expand the Crossmotor line with the larger 22-40 and 25-45; the latter was capable of delivering 52 horsepower on the belt.

1920 Case Crossmotor 15-27

SPECIFICATIONS

Crossmotor 15-27

Engine: 4-cylinder Case, vertical, transverse, overhead valve

Bore and stroke: 4.50×6.00 in.

Displacement: 382 ci., kerosene fuel

Power: 19 drawbar hp, 31 belt hp; 4-plow rating

Transmission: 2f-1r

Top speed: 3 mph

Weight: 6,460 lb.

NTTL# 4

Crossmotor 40-72

Engine: 4-cylinder Case, vertical, transverse, overhead valve

Bore and stroke: 7.00×8.00 in.

Displacement: 1,232 ci., kerosene fuel

Power: 50 drawbar hp, 91 belt hp; 8-plow rating

Transmission: 2f-1r

Top speed: 3 mph

Weight: 22,000 lb.

NTTL# 90

Case Crossmotor 40-72, built between 1920 and 1923

Case's gigantic 40-72 came out in 1920. Built on a channel steel and hot-riveted frame, it stood 9 feet tall and weighed 22,000 pounds. It was aimed at large thresher driving, prairie plowing, and road-building and earth-moving tasks. It had a 52-gallon kerosene tank and could easily consume that amount in a normal day's work. Only forty-one examples of the 40-72 were built, probably because of difficult economic times rather than a lack of usefulness.

In 1921, Case brought out the nimble 12-20 to compete directly against the popular Fordson. Case maintained that their 12-20 bested the Fordson in every respect, although it weighed 1,500 pounds more.

Crossmotor 12-20

Engine: 4-cylinder Case, vertical, transverse, overhead valve

Bore and stroke: 4.13×5.00 in.

Displacement: 267 ci., kerosene fuel

Power: 18 drawbar hp, 26 belt hp; 2-plow rating

Transmission: 2f-1r

Top speed: 3 mph

Weight: 4,450 lb.

NTTL# 91

VARIATIONS

15-27 (1919–1928), 40-72 (1920–1923), 12-20 (1921–1928)

CASE
L, LA, 500, 600, AND 900

The Case L replaced the Crossmotors 18-32 and 25-45. Designed to be competitive with the popular John Deere D, it was a standard-tread plowing tractor with a belt pulley for driving a thresher. The L was built on the unit frame concept, used a roller chain final drive—as did the Deere D—and featured a three-speed transmission and central rear PTO for powering towed implements. Rubber tires were offered in 1934, and the LI industrial version got independent turning brakes, a four-speed transmission, and electric starting.

The flagship of the Flambeau Red line of 1939 was the LA, an updated L. The engine compression ratio was raised and lubrication improved. The four-speed transmission was now included, and an electrical system was an option. The LA was offered with optional steel wheels as late as 1949. Fuel options were distillate (improved kerosene), gasoline—far and away the most common option—and LPG.

SPECIFICATIONS

L

Engine: 4-cylinder Case, vertical, inline, overhead valve

Bore and stroke: 4.625×6.000 in.

Displacement: 403 ci., kerosene fuel

Power: 45 drawbar, 37 belt hp; 4-plow rating

Transmission: 3f-1r

Top speed: 6 mph

Weight: 5,300 lb.

NTTL# 309

LA

Engine: 4-cylinder Case, vertical, inline, overhead valve

Bore and stroke: 4.625×6.000 in.

Displacement: 403 ci., gasoline fuel

Power: 42 drawbar hp, 56 belt hp; 4-plow rating

Transmission: 4f-1r

Top speed: 10 mph

Weight: 7,600 lb.

NTTL# 480

Case LA, built in the 1940s

Production of the LA ended in 1952, but it was resurrected in 1953 as the 500, the first of the new three-numbered tractors. The 600 was the same as the 500, except for a new six-speed transmission and Desert Sunset paint, rather than Flambeau Red.

500 and 600

Engine: 6-cylinder Case, vertical, inline, overhead valve

Bore and stroke: 4.00×5.00 in.

Displacement: 377 ci., diesel fuel

Power: 44 drawbar hp, 64 belt hp; 5-plow rating

Transmission: 4f-1r (Model 500), 6f-1r (Model 600)

Top speed: 10 mph

Weight: 8,100 lb.

NTTL# 508

VARIATIONS

L (1928–1940), LA (1940–1953), 500 (1953–1956), 600 (1957), 900 (1957–1959)

1935 Case CC

CASE
C, D, AND S

The C, a scaled-down version of the standard-tread L, was introduced within months of the birth of the L, with a similar engine, chassis, and drivetrain. Case soon brought out the row crop version of the C, called the CC, with a tricycle front end (on the CC-3) or wide front (on the CC-4), adjustable tread widths, and independent foot brakes. Rubber tires, a rear PTO, and an electrical system were options. In 1935, a mechanical power implement lift was offered. Alongside the standard-tread C and row crop CC were several versions: a CI industrial version, CO for orchards, CO-VS for vineyards, CCS sugar cane model, CH high-clearance version, and CD crawler.

SPECIFICATIONS

C and CC

Engine: 4-cylinder Case, vertical, inline, overhead valve

Bore and stroke: 3.885×5.500 in.

Displacement: 260 ci., kerosene fuel

Power: 20 drawbar hp, 29 belt hp; 3-plow rating

Transmission: 3f-1r

Top speed: 5 mph

Weight: 4,200 lb.

NTTL# 167

The D and its variations replaced the C and its variations in 1939, with the introduction of the Flambeau Red series. Under the new skin was essentially the same tractor as the C, except that the rated engine speed was increased from 1,100 to 1,200 rpm. Row crop DC-3 and DC-4 variants were the same as the earlier CC-3 and CC-4. A hydraulic system was added in 1950, followed by the Eagle Hitch (Case's answer to Ford-Ferguson's three-point hitch) and LPG fuel options in 1952.

D and DC

Engine: 4-cylinder Case, vertical, inline, overhead valve

Bore and stroke: 3.88×5.50 in.

Displacement: 260 ci., distillate fuel

Power: 27 drawbar hp, 32 belt hp; 3-plow rating

Transmission: 4f-1r

Top speed: 11 mph

Weight: 7,000 lb.

NTTL# 349

1939 Case DC

1954 Case SC

The S was a smaller version of the D. It was available in a complete range of versions, but the S (standard) and SC (row crop) were the largest sellers. A new short-stroke high-speed engine from Case powered the S series. In 1953, the bore was increased from 3.5 inches to 3.625 inches. Gasoline was the standard fuel, but distillate was optional.

SC

Engine: 4-cylinder Case, vertical, inline, overhead valve

Bore and stroke: 3.625×4.000 in.

Displacement: 165 ci., gasoline fuel

Power: 23 drawbar hp, 30 belt hp; 3-plow rating

Transmission: 4f-1r

Top speed: 10 mph

Weight: 5,000 lb.

NTTL# 496

VARIATIONS

C (1929–1939), CC-3 (1929–1939), CC-4 (1931–1938), D (1939–1953), DC-3 (1939–1953), DC-4 (1939–1953), S/SC (1941–1954)

1930s Case RC

CASE
RC AND R

The RC was a one-plow row crop general-purpose tractor. It featured a Waukesha four-cylinder gasoline-only engine. Tricycle and wide fronts were available, with the rear and wide front adjustable in tread widths. A rear PTO was standard, as were individual steering brakes and rubber tires. Some were built with over-engine steering and some with Case's famous "chicken-roost" steering.

A standard-tread version, the R, with the same engine and transmission, was added in 1938. For the R, fenders were standard, and the PTO was optional. The R and RC were updated in 1939 with a four-speed transmission, electrical system, and power implement lift, as well as a styling treatment that included the cast-iron "starburst" grille. RI (industrial) and RO (orchard) versions were made available at that time. The RI was equipped with electric start, foot throttle, and four-speed transmission from the start. The RO had individual brakes.

SPECIFICATIONS

RC

Engine: 4-cylinder Waukesha, vertical, inline, side valve

Bore and stroke: 3.25×4.50 in.

Displacement: 149 ci.

Power: 12 drawbar hp, 19 belt hp; 1-plow rating

Transmission: 3f-1r

Top speed: 5 mph

Weight: 3,350 lb.

NTTL# 251

VARIATIONS

RC (1935–1940), R (1938–1940)

CASE
V AND VA

The V standard, VC row crop, VI industrial, and VO orchard models all had gear final drives, rather than the chain drives used previously. An electrical system with self-starter and lights was optional.

The all-new VA series succeeded the V/VC versions. The engine and gearing were both redesigned. Initially, only a gasoline fuel system was offered, but in 1947, a distillate arrangement became an option. An extensive range of submodels was offered in the VA series, which was the first to get the Eagle Hitch (see page 35), in 1953.

(see page 35)

SPECIFICATIONS

V and VC

Engine: 4-cylinder Continental, vertical, inline, side valve

Bore and stroke: 3.00×4.38 in.

Displacement: 124 ci., gasoline fuel

Power: 15 drawbar hp, 24 belt hp; 2-plow rating

Transmission: 4f-1r

Top speed: 10 mph

Weight: 4,290 lb.

NTTL# 348

VA and VAC

Engine: 4-cylinder Case, vertical, inline, overhead cam

Bore and stroke: 3.25×3.75 in.

Displacement: 124 ci., gasoline fuel

Power: 15 drawbar hp, 20 belt hp; 1-plow rating

Transmission: 4f-1r

Top speed: 10 mph

Weight: 3,200 lb.

NTTL# 431

1948 Case VAC

1940 Case V

VARIATIONS

V Standard Tread (1940–1942), VC Row Crop (RC) (1940–1942), VO Orchard (1941–1942), VA Standard-Tread (1942–1953), VAC/VAC-12 Dual Tricycle RC (1942–1953), VAC-11 Single Front Wheel RC (1951–1953), VAC-13 Adj. Wide Front RC (1951–1953), VAC-14 Low Profile RC (1953–1954), VAO Orchard (1942–1955), VAI Industrial (1942–1955), VAO-15 Low Profile Orchard (1953–1954), VAH High Clearance (1948–1955), VAS Offset High Clearance (1952–1955)

CASE
300 AND 350

For 1955, Case introduced a completely new lineup of tractors with three-number model designations, new styling, and Desert Sunset sheet metal with Flambeau Red cast iron and wheels. The numerical system replaced the use of subletters. The 3 in 300 indicated the number of plows, the second number showed the type of fuel, and the third number was the tractor configuration. Thus, a 301 was a diesel row crop. The basic model number, 300, was decaled on the hood, but the serial number reflected the details. Two engines were available: a Case-built gasoline-distillate-LPG engine and a Continental-built diesel. Transmissions with four, eight, or twelve speeds forward were available.

The 350 came out in 1957. It was the same except that the spark ignition engines were larger in displacement, and a 12-volt electrical system was used.

1957 Case 300

SPECIFICATIONS

301

Engine: 4-cylinder Continental, vertical, inline, overhead valve

Bore and stroke: 3.38×4.38 in.

Displacement: 157 ci., diesel fuel

Power: 22 drawbar hp, 31 belt hp; 3-plow rating

Transmission: range from 4f-1r to 12f-3r

Top speed: 20 mph

Weight: 3,750 lb.

NTTL# 614

311

Engine: 4-cylinder, vertical, inline, overhead valve

Bore and stroke: 3.38×4.13 in.

Displacement: 148 ci., gasoline fuel

Power: 23 drawbar hp, 32 belt hp; 3-plow rating

Transmission: 4f-1r

Top speed: 12 mph

Weight: 3,560 lb.

NTTL# 613

VARIATIONS

300 (1955–1957), 350 (1957–1958)

CASE
400

The all-new Case 400 was available as either a standard-tread or row crop machine. It replaced the D series and came with gasoline, diesel, or LPG engines, all of the same displacement. All of the various front-end configurations were optional. The 400 featured an eight-speed transmission, a first for Case. In another departure from the past, the hand clutch (except for some specials) and chain final drive were not used. A draft-compensating three-point hitch, rubber torsion-suspension seat, and full instrumentation topped the list of features.

1957 Case 400 High Crop

SPECIFICATIONS

SPECIFICATIONS

401

Engine: 4-cylinder Case, vertical, inline, overhead valve

Bore and stroke: 4.00×5.00 in.

Displacement: 251 ci., diesel fuel

Power: 35 drawbar hp, 49 PTO hp; 4-plow rating

Transmission: 8f-2r

Top speed: 14 mph

Weight: 6,600 lb.

NTTL# 565

411

Engine: 4-cylinder Case, vertical, inline, overhead valve

Bore and stroke: 4.00×5.00 in.

Displacement: 251 ci., gasoline fuel

Power: 36 drawbar hp, 51 belt hp; 4-plow rating

Transmission: 8f-2r

Top speed: 14 mph

Weight: 6,320 lb.

NTTL# 566

VARIATIONS

400 (all versions 1955–1957)

Deere

Moline, Illinois

The acorn of John Deere's majestic oak was a single walk-behind plow, hammered out of a steel saw blade by John Deere himself in 1837 in his Grand Detour, Illinois, blacksmith shop. This simple implement was central to agricultural development in the American Midwest in the last half of the nineteenth century. From these humble roots, by scrupulous attention to making quality products and by catering to customer needs, this family-managed (until 1960) company grew into the foremost agricultural equipment manufacturer in the world.

Shortly after the turn of the twentieth century, companies such as J. I. Case, International Harvester, and Massey-Harris were developing lines of "gas" tractors. Deere, however, was slow to enter the tractor business. Concerns of risking the family fortune stood in the way, as did concerns that competing in tractors might hurt their plow business. However, since the others were now offering plows as well as tractors, Deere was compelled to respond.

JOHN DEERE
WATERLOO BOY
R AND N

Starting as early as 1912, several Deere in-house tractor designs were tried. They came to naught. In 1918, the Waterloo Gasoline Engine Company, producer of the popular Waterloo Boy tractor, became available for purchase; Deere snapped it up and was instantly in the tractor business. The Waterloo company's R was in production at the time, as was an improved N, with a larger engine and a two-speed transmission replacing the single-speed unit.

1924 John Deere Waterloo Boy N

SPECIFICATIONS
Waterloo Boy R

Engine: 2-cylinder, horizontal, side-by-side, overhead valve

Bore and stroke: 6.00×7.00 in.

Displacement: 396 ci.

Power: 11 drawbar hp, 22 belt hp; 2-plow rating

Transmission: 1f-1r

Top speed: 2.5 mph

Weight: 5,900 lb.

Waterloo Boy N

Engine: 2-cylinder, horizontal, side by side, overhead valve

Bore and stroke: 6.50×7.00 in.

Displacement: 465 ci.

Power: 12 drawbar hp, 25 belt hp; 3-plow rating

Transmission: 2f-1r

Top speed: 3.0 mph

Weight: 6,480 lb.

NTTL# 1

VARIATIONS
R (1914–1918), N (1917–1924)

1931 John Deere GP

JOHN DEERE
C, GP, AND GPWT

In the 1920s, Deere worked on motor cultivators. Although those didn't pan out, the work done was the basis for an all-purpose experimental tractor, built in 1926. Improved versions led to what became known as the C in 1927. The C was renamed the GP ("general purpose") in 1928 because "C" and "D" sounded so similar, especially on telephones of the time. The GP used an arched front axle in order to straddle the center of three rows for crop cultivation.

In 1930, a tricycle version was introduced, called the GPWT, or GP Wide-Tread—a concession to farmers who didn't take to the three-row concept. These received engines with a bore diameter increased by 0.25 inches. The engine had lower compression and did not use water injection. Also in 1930, GPWTs were converted to a GP-P (potato) configuration, with a 68-inch rear-wheel tread. The following year, improvements made for the GPWT were incorporated into the rest of the GP line, to which the GPO (orchard) had been added.

1928 John Deere GP

SPECIFICATIONS
1928 GP

Engine: 2-cylinder, horizontal, side-by-side, side valve (L-head)

Bore and stroke: 5.75×6.00 in.

Displacement: 312 ci., kerosene fuel

Power: 17 drawbar hp, 25 belt hp; 2-plow rating

Transmission: 3f-1r

Top speed: 4 mph

Weight: 3,600 lb.

NTTL# 153

1931 GP

Engine: 2-cylinder, horizontal, side-by-side, side valve

Bore and stroke: 6.00×6.00 in.

Displacement: 339 ci., distillate fuel

Power: 18.86 drawbar hp, 25.36 belt hp; 3-plow rating

Transmission: 3f-1r

Top speed: 4.25 mph

Weight: 4,925 lb.

NTTL# 190

VARIATIONS
C, GP, GPWT, GP-P, GPO (all variations 1928–1935)

JOHN DEERE
A, 60, 620, AND 630

Features of the 1934 A tractor included a new overhead-valve engine, a straight axle for splined rear-wheel adjustment, all-gear final drive, over-engine steering, and a four-speed transmission. A revolutionary new feature of the A was its built-in hydraulic pump and implement lift. The A received Dreyfuss styling treatment in 1938. (Henry Dreyfuss was a pioneer industrial designer whose New York firm exerted lasting influence on Deere products.) As from 1938 through 1946 are known as early styled (previous As were considered "unstyled"), while those produced from 1947 to 1952, with a pressed steel frame and bench seat, are known as late styled. A standard version of the A was designated AR. (The terms "regular" or "standard" were used to designate conventional, non–row crop general purpose tractors.)

In 1952, Deere changed from letter designators to two numbers. The A became the 60, with engine improvements giving a 10 percent power increase. Besides distillate and gasoline fuels, LPG was now offered. The 60 also offered live hydraulics and optional live PTO, an optional three-point hitch, power steering (1954), rack-and-pinion rear-wheel adjust, a 12-volt electrical system, and a longer clutch lever. There were two versions of the

SPECIFICATIONS

A (Steel)

Engine: 2-cylinder, horizontal, side by side, overhead valve

Bore and stroke: 5.50×6.50 in.

Displacement: 309 ci., kerosene fuel

Power: 18.72 drawbar hp, 24.71 belt hp; 2-plow rating

Transmission: 4f-1r

Top speed: 6.25 mph

Weight: 6,410 lb.

NTTL# 222

ABOVE 1934 John Deere A (Steel)

60 Standard: high seat and low seat. The low seat was a slightly restyled and upgraded AR; the high seat was built on a row crop frame.

The next iteration, the 620, came along in 1956, with yellow side panels and a draft-control three-point hitch called the Custom Powr-Trol. A 20 percent power increase came mostly through an increase in engine rpm. In the last months of production in 1958, further advances included optional power-adjustable rear wheels and steering improvements. The Orchard 620 was much the same as the Orchard 60, which was basically an AO. For the 620, however, the new engine and drivetrain components were used. The 620-O continued to be in production through the 630 years, until production of the two-cylinder line ended in 1960. In 1961, Deere switched to three-, four-, and six-cylinder engines, discontinuing the two-cylinder tradition that had started with the Waterloo Boy.

The 630 was the last of the line, debuting in August 1958. Power was the same, but improvements in operator convenience and a new four-light headlight system meant increased productivity. New features included the "Oval-Tone" muffler, optional "Float Ride" seat (a Deere-trademarked seat featuring suspension and adjustability), and optional 1,000-rpm PTO. All configurations offered for the A were maintained. The distillate and LPG versions are rare now, but they were offered throughout the life of the series.

A (Rubber)

Engine: 2-cylinder, horizontal, side-by-side, overhead valve

Bore and stroke: 5.50×6.75 in.

Displacement: 321 ci., distillate fuel

Power: 24.64 drawbar hp, 28.93 belt hp; 2-plow rating

Transmission: 4f-1r

Top speed: 6.25 mph

Weight: 6,410 lb.

NTTL# 335

VARIATIONS

A (various serial numbers from 1934–1952), 60 (1952–1956), 620 (1957–1959), 630 (1959–1960)

BELOW 1950 John Deere A (Rubber)

JOHN DEERE
B, 50, 520, AND 530

The John Deere B was the most popular of the two-cylinder tractors, with more than three hundred thousand sold. It was a smaller, cheaper running mate to the A, with all the features of the A. These included a hydraulic lift option, adjustable wheel tread, and all the various front-end configurations. The B could also be obtained in standard-tread and orchard versions, and in an orchard crawler version modified by the Lindeman brothers of Yakima, Washington.

The B became the 50 with the introduction of the two-number series. Styling was updated to give the line a "postwar" image. There were improvements too: the engine was the same, but a new two-barrel carburetor and internal improvements gave 10 percent more power. Live hydraulics and PTO were added, as were rack-and-pinion rear-wheel adjustment and an optional three-point lift.

The 520, with 20 percent more power, had new yellow sheet-metal side panels. The engine, though the same displacement, was completely new. The compression ratio was raised to increase the horsepower.

The 530 incorporated ergonomic and styling improvements. All of the tractors in this series were available in distillate, LPG, and gasoline fuel versions and all manner of front-end configurations.

SPECIFICATIONS

1947 B

Engine: 2-cylinder, horizontal, side-by-side, overhead valve

Bore and stroke: 4.69×5.50 in.

Displacement: 190 ci., gasoline fuel

Power: 19.99 drawbar hp, 25.79 belt hp; 2-plow rating

Transmission: 6f-1r

Top speed: 10.0 mph

Weight: 4,400 lb.

NTTL# 380

VARIATIONS

B (1935–1952), 50 (1952–1956), 520 (1956–1958), 530 (1958–1960)

1950 John Deere B

JOHN DEERE
G, 70, 720,
AND 730

Soon after the G entered the field in 1937, complaints arose about overheating. A recall was issued, and a taller radiator was supplied, with a notch in the top for the steering shaft to pass through. The G received Dreyfuss styling in 1942. In order to get a wartime price increase, the model designation was changed to GM ("modernized"); with wartime restrictions removed, the model reverted to G in 1947. At that time, GN ("narrow" front) and GW ("wide" front) configurations were added.

The final version of the G came out in 1947, with the pan seat replaced by a bench with a backrest. The G became the 70 in 1953 with the change to the two-number system. The 70 was originally offered in distillate, gasoline, or LPG versions, but in 1954, a diesel was added.

The 720 was an upgrade of the 70, offering Custom Powr-Trol, Deere's adaptation of the draft-control three-point hitch. The differences between the 720 and 730 were in the areas of improved ergonomics and the more rounded Dreyfuss styling. The 730 was so popular that production continued for export until March 1961. Production continued in Argentina through 1968.

1938 John Deere G

SPECIFICATIONS

G

Engine: 2-cylinder, horizontal, side-by-side, overhead valve

Bore and stroke: 6.13×7.00 in.

Displacement: 412.5 ci., distillate fuel

Power: 25.86 drawbar hp, 34.09 belt hp; 3-plow rating

Transmission: 4f-1r

Top speed: 6.00 mph

Weight: 4,480 lb.

NTTL# 295

720 (Diesel)

Engine: 2-cylinder, horizontal, side-by-side, overhead valve

Bore and stroke: 6.13×6.37 in.

Displacement: 376.0 ci., diesel fuel

Power: 40.41 drawbar hp, 56.66 belt hp; 4-plow rating

Transmission: 6f-1r

Top speed: 11.50 mph

Weight: 6,561 lb.

NTTL# 594

VARIATIONS

G (1937–1938, 1939–1940, 1947–1953), GM (1941–1946), 70 (1953–1956), 720 (1957–1958), 730 (1958–1961)

1939 John Deere H

JOHN DEERE
H

The John Deere H was essentially a scale model of the G. As a cost-saving measure, the traditional side-by-side horizontal two-cylinder engine had the power extracted from the camshaft rather than the crankshaft. To get the desired horsepower, the engine had a rated speed of 1,400 rpm. By using the camshaft, this became 700 rpm, more adaptable to the Deere tractor design and for belt pulley power transmission. To save the cost of a road gear, a governor override gas pedal was added, and in third gear, 1,800 rpm was available, yielding about 8 miles per hour. Submodels were made available, including adjustable wide front, single front wheel, and high crops, in addition to the standard tricycle row crop.

SPECIFICATIONS
1939 H

Engine: 2-cylinder, horizontal, side-by-side, overhead valve

Bore and stroke: 3.56×5.00 in.

Displacement: 99.7 ci., kerosene fuel

Power: 11.67 drawbar hp, 14.22 belt hp; 1-plow rating

Transmission: 3f-1r

Top speed: 7.75 mph

Weight: 3,035 lb.

NTTL# 312

VARIATIONS
H (1939–1947)

JOHN DEERE
62, L, AND LA

Originated by engineers at Dubuque Wagon Works in Dubuque, Iowa, rather than the Waterloo tractor operation, the 62, L, and LA were unlike previous Deere tractors. The Wagon Works engineers, not constrained by Waterloo's traditions, began with a two-cylinder Novo engine inline (not cross-mounted) and a A Ford car transmission (and steering wheel) to make a Y prototype. This was refined into the 62, with a Deere transmission and Hercules engine. The 62 had the distinction of having a "JD" logo under the radiator grille.

The 1937 model year brought the production of the L, with a Hercules engine. In late 1938, the L received Dreyfuss styling. Starting in 1941, the more powerful, heavier LA was added to the line, produced simultaneously with the L. The L, from serial number 625000 on, and the LA used a Deere-built engine. They used gasoline fuel only.

The LI industrial model of the L had a lower, wider stance. A longer axle tube was used in front, with shorter kingpins. Extensions inside the rear wheels facilitated a wider rear axle.

SPECIFICATIONS

L

Engine: 2-cylinder, vertical, side-by-side, side valve

Bore and stroke: 3.25×4.00 in.

Displacement: 66.0 ci., gasoline fuel

Power: 7.06 drawbar hp, 10.42 belt hp; 1-plow rating

Transmission: 3f-1r

Top speed: 6.00 mph

Weight: 2,180 lb.

NTTL# 313

LA

Engine: 2-cylinder, vertical, side-by-side, side valve

Bore and stroke: 3.25×4.00 in.

Displacement: 76.0 ci., gasoline fuel

Power: 10.62 drawbar hp, 14.34 belt hp; 1-plow rating

Transmission: 3f-1r

Top speed: 9.00 mph

Weight: 2,285 lb.

NTTL# 373

VARIATIONS

62 (1937), L (1937–1941), LI (1938–1946), LA (1941–1946)

TOP LEFT 1939 John Deere L

BOTTOM LEFT 1941 John Deere LA

M, 40, 320, AND 330

The M replaced the L, LA, and H. It used a vertical two-cylinder engine and a foot clutch and was built in the utility configuration, with a three-point hydraulic lift system. In 1947, Deere bought out the Lindeman brothers and began building the MC Crawler. Another variation of the M was the MT (for "tricycle"). A unique feature of the M and MT was a telescoping steering column, enabling the driver to stand. They also had a backrest seat with an air-bladder seat cushion.

With the two-number system, the M became the 40. Engine power was increased and four new versions added: the 40U – Utility, 40V – Special, 40H – High Crop, and 40W – Two-Row Utility. All versions of the 40 reverted to a regular cushion, sliding seat, and fixed steering wheel.

The next iteration was the 320. It came in standard and utility versions and was available with draft-control hydraulics. The 330 was the same as the 320 but with ergonomic improvements.

SPECIFICATIONS

M

Engine: 2-cylinder, vertical, side-by-side, overhead valve

Bore and stroke: 4.00×4.00 in.

Displacement: 100.5 ci., gasoline fuel

Power: 10.00 drawbar hp, 19.49 belt hp; 2-plow rating

Transmission: 4f-1r

Top speed: 10.0 mph

Weight: 2,695 lb.

NTTL# 387

40

Engine: 2-cylinder, vertical, side-by-side, overhead valve

Bore and stroke: 4.00×4.00 in.

Displacement: 100.5 ci., gasoline fuel

Power: 17.43 drawbar hp, 23.51 belt hp; 2-plow rating

Transmission: 4f-1r

Top speed: 12.0 mph

Weight: 3,219 lb.

NTTL# 503

VARIATIONS

M (1947–1952), MT (1949–1952), MC (1949–1952), 40 (1953–1955), 320 (1956–1958), 330 (1958–1960)

1953 John Deere 40

1948 John Deere M

1958 John Deere 420 HC

JOHN DEERE
420, 430, 435,
AND 440

The 420 replaced the 40. Distillate versions were continued, but an LPG option was added in 1958, and a water pump replaced the thermocycle cooling system. The same seven configurations as those of the 40 were offered for the 420. Other variations included an optional five-speed transmission, four-speed transmission option with shuttle shift, three-point hitch for the crawler, live PTO option, and power steering. The 1958 models got a slant steering wheel. Except for ergonomic improvements, the 430 was virtually identical to the 420.

New for 1958 was the 440, an industrial version of the 430. It was heavier and generally painted Highway Yellow, but under the skin it was the same. It was available as a 440C crawler; some 440Cs were equipped with a General Motors (GM) two-cylinder, two-cycle diesel. The agricultural 435, made in 1959 only, was the 440 mated to a General Motors two-cylinder, two-cycle diesel, equipped with a three-point hitch with draft control and a PTO. Options included power steering, five-speed transmission, and a 1,000-rpm PTO.

SPECIFICATIONS

420

Engine: 2-cylinder, vertical, side-by-side, overhead valve

Bore and stroke: 4.25×4.00 in.

Displacement: 113.0 ci., gasoline fuel

Power: 20.82 drawbar hp, 27.25 belt hp; 2-plow rating

Transmission: 4f-1r

Top speed: 12.0 mph

Weight: 3,591 lb.

NTTL# 599

435

Engine: 2-cylinder, 2-cycle, vertical, side-by-side, overhead exhaust valve

Bore and stroke: 3.88×4.50 in.

Displacement: 106.4 ci., diesel fuel

Power: 27.59 drawbar hp, 32.91 belt hp; 3-plow rating

Transmission: 5f-1r

Top speed: 13.5 mph

Weight: 4,101 lb.

NTTL# 716

VARIATIONS

420 (1956–1958), 430 (1958–1960), 435 (1959), 440 (1958–1960)

JOHN DEERE
R, 80, 820,
AND 830

The R was the follow-on to the D standard tread. With this tractor, Deere propelled itself into the diesel business. After a five-year run (1949–1954), the R was replaced by the 80 in the two-number series.

The 80 looked much the same, but the round flywheel cover of the R became a teardrop shape on the 80. The 80 engine was enlarged to increase power, and the thermocycle cooling system was changed to the water-pump type. A V-4 starter motor replaced the two-cylinder starter of the R. The 80 was the first Deere tractor to offer a factory cab.

The next iteration was the 820. The only external difference was its yellow side panels. There were improved brakes and steering and a new cab with better sealing and sound proofing. For the 1958 model year, engine improvements put the power over 75 horsepower.

The John Deere 830 had the same power as the 820. The Dreyfuss industrial design team made cosmetic and ergonomic improvements.

SPECIFICATIONS

R

Engine: 2-cylinder, horizontal, side-by-side, overhead valve

Bore and stroke: 5.75×8.00 in.

Displacement: 416 ci., diesel fuel

Power: 34.45 drawbar hp, 51.00 belt hp; 4-plow rating

Transmission: 5f-1r

Top speed: 11.5 mph

Weight: 7,603 lb.

NTTL# 406

820

Engine: 2-cylinder, horizontal, side-by-side, overhead valve

Bore and stroke: 6.13×8.00 in.

Displacement: 471.5 ci., diesel fuel

Power: 53.16 drawbar hp, 75.6 belt hp; 6-plow rating

Transmission: 6f-1r

Top speed: 12.25 mph

Weight: 7,855 lb.

NTTL# 632

VARIATIONS

R (1949–1954), 80 (1955–1965), 820 (1957–1958), 830 (1958–1960)

1958 John Deere 820 Diesel

1951 John Deere R

JOHN DEERE
8010 AND 8020

The secrecy surrounding the New Generation line of John Deere tractors, with multicylinder engines and a four-number identification system, was so complete that it seems no one picked up on the clues before the gigantic 8010 was unveiled in 1959. No one seemed to notice that Deere had jumped not just from a two- to four-cylinder engine, but to six—and not just to 100 horsepower, but to more than 200. To minimize development costs, Deere had adapted heavy-duty truck components: a GM 6-71 two-cycle engine and nine-speed transmission. Unfortunately, the transmission overheated in tractor duty. This and other problems led to a recall of all but a few 8010s. The recalled tractors were rebuilt as 8020 models.

The 8020 was up to John Deere's usual standards of quality and dependability, but the $30,000 price tag was a problem for farmers; the next smallest offering, the 4020, cost about $5,000. Yet the 8020 could do a lot of work. Deere said it could do the work of five lesser tractors (and drivers). It was equipped with a category 5 three-point hitch, had dual remote hydraulic systems, and, like the 8010, had air brakes, a hydraulically actuated clutch, and power steering through the center pivot.

SPECIFICATIONS

8020

Engine: 6-cylinder, 2-cycle, vertical, inline, overhead exhaust valve

Bore and stroke: 4.25×5.00 in.

Displacement: 426.0 ci., diesel fuel

Power: 150 drawbar hp, 215 PTO hp; 8-plow rating

Transmission: 8f-1r

Top speed: 18 mph

Weight: 24,700 lb.

VARIATIONS

8010/8020 (1959–1964)

John Deere 8020

JOHN DEERE
1010 AND 1020

The 1010 was essentially a 430 with a four-cylinder engine. It could be equipped with either a gasoline or diesel engine, the latter of the glow plug start variety. A live PTO and a Float Ride seat were options, as was a dual remote hydraulic system. For 1962, an orchard tractor was added to the line.

The 1020 replaced the 1010 in 1965. The 1020 was not a warmed-over 430 but rather a clean-sheet design. Engines now had only three cylinders, and the diesels were direct injection instead of glow plug. An eight-speed transmission was provided, with four reverse ratios. In 1967, a power shift auxiliary was added. There were also a shuttle shift option and optional dual 540/1,000 rpm PTO, rear and/or midships. Other options included an adjustable-tread swept-back front axle in place of a straight adjustable axle, various tire options, differential lock, power steering, a deluxe seat, rack-and-pinion rear-wheel adjusters, power-adjustable rear wheels, a foot throttle, Roll-Gard ROPS (roll-over protection structure), and even a belt pulley.

John Deere 1010 RS

SPECIFICATIONS
1010

Engine: 4-cylinder, vertical, inline, overhead valve

Bore and stroke: 3.63×3.50 in.

Displacement: 144.5 ci., diesel fuel

Power: 29.16 drawbar hp, 35.99 belt hp; 3-plow rating

Transmission: 5f-1r

Top speed: 16.9 mph

Weight: 3,923 lb.

NTTL# 803

1020

Engine: 3-cylinder, vertical, inline, overhead valve

Bore and stroke: 3.86×4.33 in.

Displacement: 152.0 ci., diesel fuel

Power: 31.86 drawbar hp, 38.92 belt hp; 3-plow rating

Transmission: 16f-8r

Top speed: 17.1 mph

Weight: 4,260 lb.

NTTL# 935

VARIATIONS

1010 (1961–1965), 1020 (1965–1973)

JOHN DEERE
2010 AND 2020

The four-cylinder 2010 replaced the two-cylinder 630. There were gasoline, LPG, and diesel fuel options, and all used an eight-speed transmission with optional shuttle shift, or a two-speed power shift auxiliary. The diesel was of the glow plug variety. All New Generation diesels (see page 58) had only the electric starting option. An agricultural crawler came out in 1963 but was dropped in 1964.

The 2020 replaced the 2010 in 1965. Tricycle row crops were eliminated from the lineup. The 2020 was available in three utility configurations, one of which could be ordered with orchard trim. New gasoline and direct-injection diesel engines with balance shafts were made for the 2020. Transmission options were carried over from the 2010. Power steering was standard equipment. Optional equipment included a two-speed PTO, a midship PTO, power-adjustable rear wheels, remote hydraulics, a foot throttle, and the Roll-Gard ROPS.

1965 John Deere 2020

SPECIFICATIONS

2010

Engine: 4-cylinder, vertical, inline, overhead valve

Bore and stroke: 3.88×3.50 in.

Displacement: 165 ci., diesel fuel

Power: 39.28 drawbar hp, 46.67 belt hp; 4-plow rating

Transmission: 8f-4r

Top speed: 19.3 mph

Weight: 5,054 lb.

NTTL# 799

2020

Engine: 4-cylinder, vertical, inline, overhead valve

Bore and stroke: 3.86×4.33 in.

Displacement: 202.7 ci., diesel fuel

Power: 45.90 drawbar hp, 54.09 belt hp; 4-plow rating

Transmission: 8f-4r

Top speed: 17.3 mph

Weight: 5,500 lb.

NTTL# 938

VARIATIONS

2010 (1961–1965), 2020 (1965–1971)

JOHN DEERE
2510 AND 2520

Only in America was there a demand for tricycle-front tractors. To fill that niche, Deere decided to put a 2020 engine in a 3020 chassis (see page 65) to make the 2510, aimed directly at the smaller American row crop farmer. Only row crop and Hi-Crop versions were offered, and only with gasoline or diesel engines. The two transmission choices were the Synchro-Range or Power Shift, both eight-speed units. Standard equipment included power steering, power brakes, fenders with lights, and a deluxe seat. Options were the three-point hitch, live 540/1,000-rpm rear PTO, front PTO (1,000 rpm), and a differential lock.

The 2520 engines received a displacement increase and a power bump of about 10 horsepower. Hydraulic controls moved from the left side of the dash to the right side of the seat; this location had become more or less standard for the industry. Another option for the 2520 was the ROPS, available either with or without a canopy, or a factory cab.

1966 John Deere 2510

SPECIFICATIONS

2510

Engine: 4-cylinder, vertical, inline, overhead valve

Bore and stroke: 3.86×4.33 in.

Displacement: 202.7 ci., diesel fuel

Power: 46.82 drawbar hp, 54.96 belt hp; 4-plow rating

Transmission: 8f-3r

Top speed: 15.8 mph

Weight: 6,525 lb.

NTTL# 916

2520

Engine: 4-cylinder, vertical, inline, overhead valve

Bore and stroke: 4.02×4.33 in.

Displacement: 219.8 ci., diesel fuel

Power: 55.86 drawbar hp, 61.29 belt hp; 5-plow rating

Transmission: 8f-3r

Top speed: 15.8 mph

Weight: 7,180 lb.

NTTL# 992

VARIATIONS

2510 (1966–1968), 2520 (1969–1972)

JOHN DEERE
4010 AND 4020

The 4010, top of the New Generation series, could be obtained as a row crop, standard, high crop, or industrial configuration. In row crops, there were dual tricycle, wide front, and single front-wheel arrangements. The 4010's major features were the new six-cylinder engine, a central hydraulic system, an eight-speed Synchro-Range transmission, an ergonomically designed platform, and an orthopedic seat, which provided a soft ride, and back support and was adjustable for height and leg space. For standing operation, the seat could slide up and back to be out of the way. The new central hydraulic system design featured a variable-displacement pump for raising implements, power steering, power brakes, and a differential lock.

A general upgrade of the 4010 resulted in the new 4020. Changes in 1966 included a 12-volt alternator electrical system and Roll-Gard ROPS (roll-over protection structure). A Front Wheel Assist system became available, and engine improvements increased the horsepower. The eight-speed Synchro-Range transmission remained standard equipment, but the Power Shift transmission was optional.

SPECIFICATIONS

4010

Engine: 6-cylinder, vertical, inline, overhead valve

Bore and stroke: 4.13×4.75 in.

Displacement: 380 ci., diesel fuel

Power: 71.93 drawbar hp, 84.00 PTO hp; 6-plow rating

Transmission: 8f-2r

Top speed: 14.3 mph, 18 mph with gov. o'ride

Weight: 7,100 lb.

NTTL# 761

4020

Engine: 6-cylinder, vertical, inline, overhead valve

Bore and stroke: 4.25×4.75 in.

Displacement: 404 ci., diesel fuel

Power: 83.79 drawbar hp, 94.88 PTO hp; 8-plow rating

Transmission: 8f-2r

Top speed: 17.6 mph, 20 mph with gov. o'ride

Weight: 8,100 lb.

NTTL# 930

VARIATIONS

4010 (1961–1963), 4020 (1964–1972)

LEFT 1969 John Deere 4020 High Crop

BELOW 1962 John Deere 4010

TOP John Deere 3010, built between 1961 and 1963

RIGHT 1964 John Deere 3020 Gas

JOHN DEERE
3010 AND 3020

The John Deere 3010 was essentially a scaled down four-cylinder version of the six-cylinder 4010, with many of the same features. The closed-center hydraulic system provided three circuits powered by a variable-displacement pump. One circuit was for the rockshaft or three-point hitch and remote implements; one was for power brakes; and the third was for full hydraulic power steering. (No mechanical connection existed between the steering wheel and front wheels.) The 3010 engines had the same bore and stroke as the 4010 engines but with two fewer cylinders. The transmission was the new Synchro-Range unit, which offered, in each of four ranges, gear changes in both forward and reverse without declutching. An independent hand clutch engaged a live 540/1,000-rpm rear PTO. Changing stub shafts produced the desired output speed. The mid-PTO operated at 1,000 rpm only.

New for the 1961 tractors was a 12-volt electrical system with an alternator. Diesels used a two-battery 24-volt starter. Also new was a foot throttle with a governor override, which could be used to get extra highway speed.

The 3020 was much the same as the 3010 it replaced in 1964, but it had a bit more power, with optional Power Shift transmission and optional Front Wheel Assist (made available in 1968). In 1969, Deere gave the gasoline and LPG engines a substantial displacement increase. The 3020's diesel was holding its own and remained the same displacement but with internal improvements. A general upgrade in 1969, in areas besides the engine, kept the 3020 on the cutting edge. A new console on the right side of the driver was a great improvement in ergonomics, and the new optional Power Shift transmission offered eight speeds forward, four in reverse. The standard transmission was the Synchro-Range unit. Also available as an option was a differential lock. The 3020 was available in three configurations: row crop, standard, and row crop utility/orchard.

SPECIFICATIONS

3010

Engine: 4-cylinder, vertical, inline, overhead valve

Bore and stroke: 4.13×4.75 in.

Displacement: 254 ci., diesel fuel

Power: 52.77 drawbar hp, 59.44 belt hp; 5-plow rating

Transmission: 8f-4r

Top speed: 14.5 mph, 18 mph with gov. o'ride

Weight: 5,568 lb.

NTTL# 762

3020

Engine: 4-cylinder, vertical, inline, overhead valve

Bore and stroke: 4.25×4.75 in.

Displacement: 270 ci., diesel fuel

Power: 61.47 drawbar hp, 71.26 belt hp; 6-plow rating

Transmission: 8f-4r

Top speed: 17.6 mph, 20 mph with gov. o'ride

Weight: 7,610 lb.

NTTL# 940

VARIATIONS

3010 (1961–1963), 3020 (1964–1972)

Ford

Dearborn, Michigan

"I want to lift the burden of farming from flesh and bones and place it on steel and motors," said auto magnate Henry Ford when he launched his famous Fordson tractor in 1917. He was fifty-three years old by then and on his way to becoming one of the richest men in the world, with his assembly line–produced T automobile. Even so, in 1938, Irishman Harry Ferguson bluntly told Ford that he didn't have enough money to buy Ferguson's three-point implement system patents— patents that had the potential, both men recognized, to revolutionize power farming. So the two agreed to build a tractor together—the Ford-Ferguson— on the basis of a handshake, to replace the Fordson (which, by then, had been discontinued in the United States).

1924 Fordson F

FORDSON
F, N, ALL-AROUND, AND E27N

The Fordson F was the culmination of years of experimenting by Ford and his engineers, starting in 1907. But it took the impetus of a World War I order to spur them into action and commit their latest design to production. Production began in late 1917 on tractors for the British Ministry of Munitions. These were built under a company separate from the Ford Motor Company, called Henry Ford and Son—the name signifying the inclusion of Henry's only son, Edsel, in the tractor company. At first, the tractor had no name, but for trans-Atlantic cable communications, "Henry Ford and Son" was shortened to "Fordson," and that name was later applied to the production tractors.

US Fordson production was discontinued in 1928, transferred to Ireland, and shortly thereafter moved to Dagenham, England. At the time of the transfer to Ireland, the Fordson was given a modernizing upgrade and renamed the N. The N was heavier and better balanced, with more power. A row crop version of the N, designated the Fordson All-Around, was exported to the United States.

SPECIFICATIONS

F

Engine: 4-cylinder, vertical, inline, side valve

Bore and stroke: 4.00×5.00 in.

Displacement: 251 ci., kerosene fuel

Power: 10 drawbar hp, 20 belt hp; 2-plow rating

Transmission: 3f-1r

Top speed: 7 mph

Weight: 2,700 lb.

NTTL# 18

1937 Fordson All-Around

1948 Fordson E27N

When World War II ended, there was neither time nor material available at Dagenham Ford for a completely new tractor. The British Ford Motor Company therefore undertook a modernization of the venerable Fordson. The new design was called the Fordson Major and designated the E27N ("E" for English, "27" for the horsepower, and "N," the Ford symbol for tractors). The E27N was to have more crop clearance and a three-plow rating. The engine of the Fordson N was retained. The rear axle of the E27N used spiral bevel gears, rather than the worm-drive rear end of the F and N. After 1948, a hydraulic three-point hitch was available, but draft control was not included. A Perkins P6 (TA) diesel was an option after 1950. (Perkins Engine Company Ltd. of Peterborough, England, was a pioneer in diesel engines for tractors.)

All-Around

Engine: 4-cylinder, vertical, inline, side valve

Bore and stroke: 4.13×5.00 in.

Displacement: 267 ci., distillate fuel

Power: 16 drawbar hp, 22 belt hp; 2-plow rating

Transmission: 3f-1r

Top speed: 5 mph

Weight: 4,000 lb. (steel wheels)

NTTL# 282

E27N

Engine: 4-cylinder, vertical, inline, side valve

Bore and stroke: 4.13×5.00 in.

Displacement: 267 ci., gasoline fuel

Power: 17 drawbar hp, 27 belt hp; 3-plow rating

Transmission: 3f-1r

Top speed: 8 mph

Weight: 4,500 lb. (steel wheels)

VARIATIONS

F (1918–1928), N (1929–1946), E27N (1945–1952)

FORD-FERGUSON
9N AND 2N

Ferguson developed a manual-lift plow for the Fordson that was quite successful, and he had also developed a small tractor with built-in hydraulics and an integral implement lift. Getting the little tractor into volume production by teaming with England's David Brown Company had proven to be problematic. Ferguson knew who had mastered the art of volume production, so he demonstrated his tractor and implements to Henry Ford. Ford was suitably impressed. The handshake agreement was made, and the Ford-Ferguson tractor with the three-point hitch was born. Ford would build the tractor using the Ferguson system; Ferguson would develop the implements and the dealer organization.

The tractor, designated the Ford-Ferguson 9N (9 for 1939), used a four-cylinder engine with parts from the Ford V-8. Other car and truck parts were used where possible. In 1942, wartime shortages led to the introduction of the 2N (for 1942), with steel wheels and without a starter or generator, to save critical materials. It was not long before supplies of rubber and copper were sufficient, however, and most 2Ns were built with starters, generators, and rubber tires. They were then much the same as the 9N. Models 9/2NAN were configured for distillate fuels.

SPECIFICATIONS
9N and 2N

Engine: 4-cylinder, vertical, inline, side valve

Bore and stroke: 3.19×3.75 in.

Displacement: 119.7 ci., gasoline fuel

Power: 16 drawbar hp, 23 PTO hp; 2-plow rating

Transmission: 3f-1r (6f-2r with Sherman step-up auxiliary)

Top speed: 11 mph (18 mph with Sherman step-up auxiliary)

Weight: 2,400 lb.

NTTL# 339

VARIATIONS
9N (1939–1942), 2N (1942–1947)

1939 Ford-Ferguson 9N

1951 Ford 8N

FORD
8N

When Henry Ford died, Henry Ford II took over. He soon discovered that his company was losing money on the tractor and notified Ferguson that 1947 was to be the last year of the handshake agreement.

The Ford Dearborn Implement line was instituted, and a modernized tractor, the 8N, was produced without Ferguson. The Ford 8N (for 1948) was not all new; it retained the hydraulic system and three-point hitch of the 9N/2N. Ferguson sued, claiming patent infringement, and won. While the 8N featured the same styling and engine as the 9N and 2N, the engine's compression was raised. A four-speed gearbox replaced the previous three-speed unit. The brake system, hydraulic lift, and steering were improved. In the last year of production, a high-direct-low auxiliary transmission was an option. The 8N was painted light gray, with red castings and wheels. 8NAN tractors were the same, except for being configured for distillate fuels.

SPECIFICATIONS

8N

Engine: 4-cylinder, vertical, inline, side valve

Bore and stroke: 3.19×3.75 in.

Displacement: 119.7 ci., gasoline fuel

Power: 18 drawbar hp, 26 PTO hp; 2-plow rating

Transmission: 4f-1r (12f-3r with 3-speed auxiliary)

Top speed: 11 mph (22 mph with 3-speed auxiliary)

Weight: 2,500 lb.

NTTL# 443

VARIATIONS

8N (1947–1952)

FORDSON
NEW MAJOR, POWER MAJOR, AND SUPER MAJOR

The Fordson E27N had been named the Major; the first all-new tractor from British Ford was introduced as the "New Major." The New Major was offered in three engine configurations: distillate, gasoline, and diesel. The diesel used a larger bore, giving a displacement advantage over the spark-ignition types. It offered a three-point hitch, but not with draft control, and it used the same three-speed transmission as the E27N but included a two-range auxiliary. All were general-purpose row crops. The New Major departed from the unit frame concept and used a channel frame.

In 1958, the Power Major was introduced. It was much the same, although the distillate version was dropped. Improvements to the fuel injection system raised the diesel horsepower.

The Super Major came out in late 1960. A draft-control three-point hitch was now included, as were disk brakes and a differential lock. In 1962, Super Majors were exported to the United States in a blue-and-cream livery, labeled Ford 5000 Diesel. In the last year of production, there were some gear ratio changes, hydraulic system improvements, and a change of the color scheme. These were called "New Performance" Super Majors.

SPECIFICATIONS
New Major

Engine: 4-cylinder, vertical, inline, overhead valve

Bore and stroke: 3.74×4.52 in.

Displacement: 199 ci., gasoline fuel

Power: 24 drawbar hp, 34 belt hp; 3-plow rating

Transmission: 6f-2r

Top speed: 13 mph

Weight: 5,165 lb.

NTTL# 501

VARIATIONS

New Major (1953–1958), Power Major (1958–1961), Super Major (1961–1963), NP Super Major (1964)

1952 Fordson Major

NAA, 600, 700, 601, 701, AND 501

For 1953, the NAA replaced the 8N, which had been in production since late 1947. A round emblem on the front center of the hood proclaimed the 1953 version to be the "Golden Jubilee Model, 1903–1953"—celebrating the fiftieth anniversary of the Ford Motor Company. The 1954 version was essentially the same, except that the medallion had only four-pointed stars. It featured a new overhead-valve engine. The four-speed transmission was standard, but the ratios were different from those of the 8N, providing slower tractor speeds at the same engine rpms. The three-speed step-up, normal, step-down auxiliary was an option, giving twelve speeds forward and three in reverse.

SPECIFICATIONS

NAA, 600, and 700 Series

Engine: 4-cylinder, vertical, inline, overhead valve

Bore and stroke: 3.44×3.60 in.

Displacement: 134 ci., gasoline fuel

Power: 20 drawbar hp, 32 PTO hp; 3-plow rating

Transmission: 4f-1r or 5f-1r (12f-3r with 3-speed auxiliary)

Top speed: 11–12 mph (22 mph with 3-speed auxiliary, with 4-speed main only)

Weight: 3,000 lb.

NTTL# 494

1953 Ford NAA Jubilee

1961 Ford 601 Workmaster

The NAA hydraulic system was new, with a continuous engine-driven pump. The same three-point hitch system with draft and position control was carried forward from the 8N. A live PTO was an extra-cost option, but few were delivered with it.

The 600 series consisted at first of the 640, 650, and 660. The 640 was much the same as the 1954 NAA, although Ford claimed thirty-one improvements. The 650 and 660 had a new five-speed transmission, while the 660 was regularly equipped with a live PTO. Before the end of 1955, three more variations were added: the 620 (four-speed, no hydraulics or PTO), 630 (three-point hitch, no PTO), and 700 (row crop). The 700 had tricycle and adjustable wide fronts.

In 1957, the last digit in the model number was changed to a 1, that is, 601, 701. LPG and diesel options were added. The 10f-2r power shift Select-O-Speed became optional. A 501 row crop/offset high-clearance tractor was also added. Models 601 and 501 were given a new all-red paint scheme.

681

Engine: 4-cylinder, vertical, inline, overhead valve

Bore and stroke: 3.56×3.60 in.

Displacement: 144 ci., diesel fuel

Power: 26 drawbar hp, 32 PTO hp; 3-plow rating

Transmission: 10f-2r

Top speed: 11 mph

Weight: 3,490 lb.

NTTL# 706

VARIATIONS

NAA (1953–1954), 600 Series (1955–1957), 700 Series (1955–1957), 601 Series (1958–1961), 701 Series (1958–1961), 501 Series (1959–1961)

FORDSON
DEXTA, SUPER DEXTA, ND NEW PERFORMANCE SUPER DEXTA

In 1957, British Ford introduced an equivalent of the US Ford 600 series. It was called the Dexta, a word meaning handy or useful. A three-cylinder Perkins diesel engine powered the Dexta. (A four-cylinder gasoline version was made in very limited quantities.) A three-speed transmission with a two-speed auxiliary was used, providing six speeds forward and two in reverse. A draft-control three-point hitch was standard equipment, and live PTO and hydraulics were available. The Dexta had blue paint with red wheels.

A Super Dexta model came out in 1962. It featured a displacement increase from 144 to 153 cubic inches. Rated engine speed also increased, from 2,000 rpm to 2,250 rpm; the power rose from 32 to 39 horsepower. A differential lock was also added. The New Performance Super Dexta debuted the following year. Power was increased to 45 horsepower by increasing the rated engine speed to 2,450 rpm. These were also exported to the United States, painted beige (wheels) and blue and labeled the Ford 2000 Diesel.

This arrangement continued until 1964, when Ford embraced the "World Tractor" concept, the Fordson name was dropped, and all Ford factories worldwide began producing the same lineup of models.

SPECIFICATIONS

Dexta

Engine: 3-cylinder, vertical, inline, overhead valve

Bore and stroke: 3.50×5.00 in.

Displacement: 144 ci., diesel fuel

Power: 23 drawbar hp, 31 belt hp; 2-plow rating

Transmission: 6f-2r

Top speed: 17 mph

Weight: 3,400 lb.

NTTL# 684

VARIATIONS

Dexta (1958–1961), Super Dexta (1961–1962), New Performance Super Dexta (1962–1964)

1959 Fordson Dexta

Ford 801 Powermaster, built between 1957 and 1962

FORD
800, 900, 801, AND 901

These tractors were essentially the same as their 600–700 series counterparts, except that the engine bore was increased from 3.56 to 3.90 inches, allowing an ample 172-cubic-inch displacement and putting the 800, 900, 801, and 901 into the 40-horsepower class. Gasoline, LPG, and diesel versions were available, as was the ten-speed power shift Select-O-Speed transmission. Again, model numbers indicated the configuration: the 8 was a four-wheel utility type, the 9 a row crop. The middle numbers indicated the following:

-1-: Select-O-Speed, no PTO
-2-: four-speed, no PTO or three-point lift
-3-: four-speed, lift, but no PTO
-4-: four-speed, with lift and PTO
-5-: five-speed, lift, and nonlive PTO
-6-: five-speed, lift, and live PTO
-7-: Select-O-Speed, lift, and live PTO
-8-: Select-O-Speed, lift, and nonlive PTO

SPECIFICATIONS

800 and 900 Series

Engine: 4-cylinder, vertical, inline, overhead valve

Bore and stroke: 3.90×3.60 in.

Displacement: 172 ci., gasoline fuel

Power: 32 drawbar hp, 43 PTO hp; 3-plow rating

Transmission: 4f-1r, 5f-1r, 10f-2r (12f-3r with 3-speed auxiliary)

Top speed: 12 mph (18 mph with 3-speed auxiliary, with 4-speed main only)

Weight: 3,400 lb. (800 Series), 3,625 lb. (900 Series)

NTTL# 641

ABOVE 1958 Ford 901 Powermaster

TOP Ford 900 Row Crop, built between 1955 and 1957

801 and 901 Series

Engine: 4-cylinder, vertical, inline, overhead valve

Bore and stroke: 3.90×3.60 in.

Displacement: 172 ci., diesel fuel

Power: 29 drawbar hp, 42 PTO hp; 3-plow rating

Transmission: 4f-1r, 5f-1r, 10f-2r (12f-3r with 3-speed auxiliary)

Top speed: 12 mph (16 mph with 3-speed auxiliary, with 4-speed main only)

Weight: 3,570 lb. (801 Series), 3,825 lb. (901 Series)

NTTL# 654

VARIATIONS

800 Series (1955–1957), 900 Series (1955–1957), 801 Series (1958–1961), 901 Series (1958–1961)

FORD
6000 AND
COMMANDER
6000

The Ford 6000 was built on a frame, rather than the unit concept, and it was offered only with the ten-speed Select-O-Speed power shift transmission. Originally a diesel, a gasoline engine was soon added, and still later, an LPG-fueled version was made available. It incorporated a category 2 three-point hitch with lower-link draft sensing. The hydraulic system used an accumulator (and later, two accumulators). The hydraulic system powered the steering and disk brakes, as well as the three-point hitch. The tractor featured a unique PTO that provided 540- or 1,000-rpm outputs (driver's choice) at either of two engine speeds.

In September 1962, the new blue-and-gray World Tractors were unveiled to dealers, along with an improved 6000. Then, in 1965, the restyled, further improved, and mainly blue Commander 6000 came out. It was at this point that the LPG engine option was added to existing gasoline and diesel versions. The 10f-2r Select-O-Speed power shift transmission was still the only option. The power steering, however, now had an independent hydraulic system and pump.

SPECIFICATIONS

6000 (Diesel)

Engine: 6-cylinder, vertical, inline, overhead valve

Bore and stroke: 3.62×3.90 in.

Displacement: 242 ci., diesel fuel

Power: 45 drawbar hp, 63 PTO hp; 5-plow rating

Transmission: 10f-2r

Top speed: 18 mph

Weight: 7,165 lb.

NTTL# 843

6000 (Gasoline)

Engine: 6-cylinder, vertical, inline, overhead valve

Bore and stroke: 3.62×3.60 in.

Displacement: 223 ci., gasoline fuel

Power: 45 drawbar hp, 62 PTO hp; 5-plow rating

Transmission: 10f-2r

Top speed: 18 mph

Weight: 6,985 lb.

NTTL# 842

VARIATIONS

6000 (1961–1964), 6000 Commander (1965–1967)

1961 Ford 6000 Diesel

Massey Ferguson

Coventry, England, and Detroit, Michigan

Henry George "Harry" Ferguson was born in 1884 in Northern Ireland. Harry, who had a penchant for mechanical things, soon left farming and became an auto mechanic and racer—he even designed and flew his own airplane in 1910. In 1914 with the onset of World War I, Ferguson became involved with the British Ministry of Munitions (MOM) food production program, in which the government imported all US tractors available to stave off food shortages caused by enemy submarine warfare. In his duties for the MOM, he became familiar with tractors, especially the Fordson, which had a tendency to power itself over backwards due to its power-to-weight ratio. After the war, Ferguson assembled a team of talented mechanics to design a plow for the Fordson that prevented the rearing action. Unable to interest Ford in the plow, he built his own tractor, the first to incorporate a hydraulic three-point hitch with draft control. David Brown, an English gear maker, manufactured the tractor, known as the Ferguson-Brown Type A. Due to economic conditions in the 1930s, the tractor didn't sell well, and a falling out between Ferguson and Brown ensued. Ferguson then took the tractor to the United States and demonstrated it to Henry Ford. The result was the "handshake agreement" leading to the Ford-Ferguson 9N. All went well until Henry Ford died and Henry II took over. After examining the books, Henry II decided to abrogate the handshake agreement, and Ferguson then began manufacturing a lookalike tractor in both Detroit and England. Fierce competition followed. In 1955, Ferguson and Massey-Harris merged to form Massey Ferguson.

FERGUSON-BROWN
TYPE A

Harry Ferguson's first tractor, built in 1933, had a hydraulic three-point hitch with draft control. He used a Hercules engine with transmission and differential gears from David Brown, a gear maker in Huddersfield, England. Individual rear-wheel brakes were included, but otherwise, the tractor—which was painted black and came to be known as the "Black Tractor"—was much like a scale model of a Fordson. With this prototype used for demonstrations, Ferguson attempted to enlist a British company to commit to mass production.

While he was not successful in his attempt, he eventually worked out an agreement with Brown to build an improved version of the tractor. The first of the Ferguson-Brown Type A tractors was ready by May 1936. It was much like the Black Tractor, but it used a Coventry Climax engine in place of the Hercules and had battleship gray paint. After production of the first five hundred Type A tractors, David Brown Ltd. bought the engine patterns and built the final eight hundred or so engines.

SPECIFICATIONS

Type A

Engine: 4-cylinder, vertical, inline, side valve

Bore and stroke: 3.15×4.00 in.

Displacement: 122.7 ci., gasoline fuel

Power: 10 drawbar hp, 20 PTO hp; 2-plow rating

Transmission: 3f-1r

Top speed: 5 mph

Weight: 1,700 lb.

VARIATIONS

Black (1933), Type A (1936–1939)

1936 Ferguson-Brown A

1955 Ferguson TE-20 with TVO engine

FERGUSON
TE-20 AND TO-20

All attempts to get the Ford-Ferguson tractor produced in Britain were rebuffed, so Ferguson carried out his threat to manufacture his own version in England. No efforts were made to distinguish Ferguson's tractor: Ford drawings were adapted, tooling and stamping equipment were purchased from the same places (although Ferguson's parts were purposely not interchangeable with the Ford parts), and the same gray paint was even used. The new tractor was designated the TE-20 (tractor, England, 20 horsepower). A US-built Continental engine was used in about the first 48,000 tractors, along with a Lucas electrical system. After that, a Vanguard engine was used. The TE-20 had wheels like the 8N Ford, a tilting hood, and a shift lever–operated starter. There were numerous versions: narrow, short wheelbase, lower, kerosene, diesel, and tracked.

A Ferguson tractor plant was built in Detroit to make the TO-20 ("overseas") version, which was essentially the same as the TE-20 with the Continental engine. The main difference was the TO's use of US electrical components.

SPECIFICATIONS

TE-20

Engine: 4-cylinder, vertical, inline, overhead valve

Bore and stroke: 3.19×3.74 in.

Displacement: 119.8 ci., gasoline fuel

Power: 16 drawbar hp, 24 PTO hp; 2-plow rating

Transmission: 4f-1r

Top speed: 12 mph

Weight: 2,500 lb.

NTTL# 392

FERGUSON
TO-30, TO-35, AND 40

MASSEY FERGUSON
MF-50 AND MF-35

A new model produced in the Detroit factory starting in August 1951, the TO-30 used a larger Continental engine than that of the TO-20. Besides that, the TO-30 had an improved seat, steering, and hydraulics and a left-side clutch, with both brake pedals on the right. Otherwise, it was much the same as the TO-20.

The TO-35 came out in 1954. Its Continental engine stretched to 134 cubic inches and 32 horsepower, and it had a six-speed transmission and further improved hydraulics. In appearance, it was much the same as the Ferguson TE/TO-20, except that the paint scheme was now green and gray.

SPECIFICATIONS

Ferguson TO-30

Engine: 4-cylinder, vertical, inline, overhead valve

Bore and stroke: 3.25×3.88 in.

Displacement: 129 ci., gasoline fuel

Power: 19.26 drawbar hp, 28 PTO hp; 2-plow rating

Transmission: 4f-1r

Top speed: 12 mph

Weight: 2,800 lb.

NTTL# 466

1955 Ferguson 35

In 1953, Ferguson merged with the Massey-Harris Company, a Wisconsin- and Toronto-based agricultural equipment company (see page 112). A "Two-Line Policy" was then adopted, according to which existing lines of tractors and implements were still sold through the companies' respective dealerships.

Ferguson dealers requested a row crop tractor—in vogue in the mid-1950s—so a cosmetic adjustment was made to the Massey-Harris 50, which then became the Ferguson 40. The Ferguson 40 was introduced in 1956 with row crop capabilities. The Massey-Harris 50, Ferguson 40, and TO-35 were virtually identical, except for changes to the front axle and steering-accommodating narrow fronts. In 1957, beige-and-green livery was adopted for the Ferguson 40.

Both the Ferguson 40 and Massey-Harris 50 were phased out in 1958 with the end of the Two-Line Policy, but they were combined and continued as the Massey Ferguson 50. A Perkins diesel was an option in the MF-50. In 1955, the Ferguson TO-35 was revived as the MF-35, with a diesel option.

Massey Ferguson MF-50

Engine: 3-cylinder, vertical, inline, overhead valve

Bore and stroke: 3.60×5.00 in.

Displacement: 153 ci., diesel fuel

Power: 36 drawbar hp, 38 PTO hp; 3-plow rating

Transmission: 6f-1r

Top speed: 15 mph

Weight: 3,933 lb.

NTTL# 807

VARIATIONS

TO-30 (1951–1954), TO-35 (1954–1955), Massey Ferguson 35 (1955–1958), Ferguson 40 (1956–1958), Massey-Harris 50 (1956–1958), Massey Ferguson 50 (1958–1964)

1959 Massey Ferguson 50

1959 Massey Ferguson 65

MASSEY FERGUSON
MF-65

The MF-65 was larger than the MF-50 and had more power. It was sold in both the United States and United Kingdom. Gasoline and LPG versions used a Continental four-cylinder engine of 176 cubic inches, and a diesel version used a 204-cubic-inch four-cylinder Perkins engine. A three-speed transmission with a two-range manual shift auxiliary was used. The heritage of the Ferguson TO-35 was apparent. Gearboxes at the ends of the axles cut the torque on the familiar 35 drivetrain and adjusted the speed for larger tires.

In 1961, a Mark II version of the MF-65 was unveiled. The engine power of the diesel increased, and a differential lock became standard equipment. The Multi-Power two-speed power shift became an option, giving twelve speeds forward and four in reverse. The MF-65 was offered in row crop or utility configurations, as an orchard tractor, and in gasoline, diesel, and LPG fuels.

SPECIFICATIONS
MF-65 Mark II

Engine: 4-cylinder, vertical, inline, overhead valve

Bore and stroke: 3.60×5.00 in.

Displacement: 204 ci., diesel fuel

Power: 44 drawbar hp, 51 PTO hp; 4-plow rating

Transmission: 12f-4r

Top speed: 19 mph

Weight: 4,511 lb.

NTTL# 808

VARIATIONS

MF-65 (1957–1961), MF-65 II (1961–1965)

FERGUSON
60

MASSEY FERGUSON
MF-85, 88,
AND SUPER 90

Harry Ferguson commissioned a team in 1948 to design, build, and test the LTX ("Large Tractor Experimental"), or TO-60. At the time of the Ferguson–Massey-Harris merger in 1953, all development of LTX prototypes halted. The Massey people were not favorably disposed toward the LTX, by then known as the Ferguson 60, because it did not cater to the row crop configuration. Thus the program was terminated.

The Massey Ferguson 85 had its roots in the demise of the LTX. When that was canceled, development of a 60-horsepower machine was offered to placate those disappointed by its demise. Because of the Two-Line Policy, there was to be an FE-80 for Ferguson dealers and a MH-90 for Massey dealers; when the policy ended in 1958, the designation was changed to MF-85. Using a Continental four-cylinder engine, it was the first tractor with a five-plow rating and a draft-control three-point hitch. The 85 was available in utility and row crop configurations and gasoline or LPG versions. Disk brakes were used, along with a four-speed transmission with a two-range auxiliary, for a total of eight speeds forward and two in reverse.

Those with roots in Massey-Harris wanted to revive the MH-555, their big standard-tread plowing tractor, for the Great Plains farmers, upgrading it with the Ferguson draft-control three-point hitch and more power. An easier course was to beef up the MF-85 into a diesel wheatland plowing tractor and call it the MF-88. A 277-cubic-inch Continental diesel was used, although the 242-cubic-inch Continental gasoline engine from the 85 was an option. The MF-88 was otherwise much the same as the 85, except for bigger tires, massive fenders, and a standard-tread front axle.

SPECIFICATIONS

MF-85

Engine: 4-cylinder, vertical, inline, overhead valve

Bore and stroke: 3.88×5.13 in.

Displacement: 242 ci., gasoline fuel

Power: 51 drawbar hp, 61 PTO hp; 5-plow rating

Transmission: 8f-2r

Top speed: 19 mph

Weight: 5,737 lb.

NTTL# 726

VARIATIONS

MF-85 (1959–1961), MF-88 (1959–1961), MF Super 90 (1961–1965)

1961 Massey Ferguson 85

The Super 90 made its debut in 1962, replacing the 85 and 88 models. It was similar to the MF-88 except for its use of a 302-cubic-inch Perkins four-cylinder diesel and square-topped rear fenders. Some were equipped with a two-range power shift that yielded sixteen speeds forward and four in reverse.

MASSEY FERGUSON
MF-95, MF-97, AND MF-98

In 1958, Massey management bought tractors from other manufacturers and added Massey sheet metal (mainly the grille) and paint. The MF-95, based on the Minneapolis-Moline GBD (see page 137), was introduced in 1958 and featured an M-M six-cylinder diesel. In 1961, the M-M Gvi replaced the GBD in production, so MF-95 tractors were based on the Gvi after that. About the only difference was that the engine speed changed from 1,300 to 1,500 rpm.

The Massey Ferguson MF-97 was based on a Minneapolis-Moline G705 for the two-wheel-drive version and their G706 for the version with front-wheel assist. Both diesel and LPG versions were available. MF-98 was based on the Oliver Super 99GM (see page 151), with a Massey grille and paint. This tractor used a two-cycle, three-cylinder supercharged diesel engine built by General Motors. The MF-95 and MF-98 were not tested at the University of Nebraska (see page 7), but the M-M GBD, Gvi Diesel, and Oliver Super 99GM were.

SPECIFICATIONS
MF-95

Engine: 6-cylinder, vertical, inline, overhead valve

Bore and stroke: 4.25×5.00 in.

Displacement: 426 ci., diesel fuel

Power: 66 drawbar hp, 79 PTO hp; 6-plow rating

Transmission: 5f-1r

Top speed: 17 mph

Weight: 8,335 lb.

NTTL# 792 (M-M Gvi)

MF-97

Engine: 6-cylinder, vertical, inline, overhead valve

Bore and stroke: 4.63×5.00 in.

Displacement: 504 ci., diesel fuel

Power: 88 drawbar hp, 102 PTO hp; 6-plow rating

Transmission: 5f-1r

Top speed: 18 mph

Weight: 9,165 lb.

NTTL# 833 (M-M G706)

VARIATIONS

MF-95 (1958–1961),
MF-97 (1961–1965),
MF-98 (1959–1960)

ABOVE 1963 Massey Ferguson 97

TOP 1961 Massey Ferguson 95 Super

International Harvester

Chicago, Illinois

It boggles the mind to consider the animal and human efforts that went into producing food prior to the twentieth century. Certainly, Cyrus McCormick's reaper of 1831 was a leap forward, but it was not until the advent of dependable internal combustion tractors that things changed much.

The International Harvester Company was formed in 1902 by the merger of the McCormick Harvesting Machine Company with archrival Deering Harvester Company and five smaller implement manufacturers. International Harvester, also known as Harvester or simply IH, went on to become, at its peak, the largest, most successful truck, tractor, and agricultural implement company in the world. Tractor production began in 1906, and Harvester soon became the major player in the market. McCormick and Deering had maintained separate dealerships, so two lines of tractors were developed: the Mogul for McCormick and Titan for Deering.

But it was seldom smooth sailing for International Harvester, which was plagued by problems: management missteps, competition, economic depression, labor problems, drought in the farm belt, and difficulties obtaining working capital. After eighty-two years, the end of International Harvester came with a merger with another archrival in 1984: Case, a subsidiary of Tenneco Inc.

1911 International Harvester Titan D

INTERNATIONAL HARVESTER
TYPES A AND B, MOGUL TYPE C, AND TITAN TYPE D

The first IH tractor, the Type A (15 horsepower), was assembled in 1906 by installing a Harvester-built Famous-brand one-cylinder engine on a Morton chassis. A friction drive was used, with reverse motion selected by shifting the engine on frame rails. Later variations on the Type A theme came in 10-, 12-, and 20-horsepower sizes. By 1908, the Type A had switched to a gear drive and clutch, replacing the friction drive, but a friction reverse was still used. In 1910, a new A and a Type B (20 horsepower) were introduced, with gear reverse and two forward gears.

SPECIFICATIONS

Mogul Type C and Titan Type D

Engine: 1-cylinder, horizontal, transverse, overhead valve

Bore and stroke: 8.75×15.00 in.

Displacement: 902 ci., kerosene fuel

Power: 12 drawbar hp, 25 belt hp; 3-plow rating

Transmission: 1f-1r

Top speed: 2.0 mph

Weight: 10,000 lb.

1912 International Harvester Mogul Type C

Mogul-brand IH tractors were made for McCormick dealers; Titans were made for separate Deering dealers. The Titan Type D was introduced in 1910 and was much the same as 1911's Mogul Type C. All used the same Famous engine. Shortly after production began on the Type D, a cubical cooling-tower design replaced the evaporation-type cooling system, differentiating early Titans from Moguls. An improved Type D was built between 1912 and 1915, rated at 35 belt and 18 drawbar horsepower.

Several other Mogul and Titan tractors were built using the same basic configuration, with single- and two-cylinder engines.

VARIATIONS

Mogul Type A (1907–1916), Mogul Junior (1911–1913), Mogul 45 (1911–1917), Mogul 30-60 (1911–1917), Mogul Type C (1911–1914), Titan Type D (1910–1914), Titan 45 (1911–1915), Titan 18-35 (1912–1915), Titan 30-60 (1915–1917)

INTERNATIONAL HARVESTER
MOGUL 8-16, MOGUL 10-20, AND TITAN 10-20

The Mogul 8-16 was a substantial tractor, built from 1914 to 1917, with 14,000 made—a number exceeding all previous IH tractors combined. An improved version, the Mogul 10-20, was also produced during 1916 and 1917. In 1915, the Titan 10-20, a similar tractor, was made for Deering dealers. All of these tractors used a gooseneck frame, with close-set front wheels for sharper turning and ample clearance for the flat belt.

The Titan 10-20 featured a two-cylinder engine with horizontal side-by-side cylinders, with the pistons operating in unison. While it had the same type of frame as the Mogul, it used automotive-type steering, rather than the over-the-engine type with a worm and sector gear used on the Mogul. The Mogul used hopper cooling with a water pump; the Titan used a thermosyphon cooling system, which relied on gravity for water circulation. The Titan outsold Mogul versions by a wide margin.

SPECIFICATIONS

Mogul 8-16

Engine: 1-cylinder, horizontal, transverse, overhead valve

Bore and stroke: 8.00×12.00 in.

Displacement: 603 ci., kerosene fuel

Power: 8 drawbar hp, 16 belt hp; 2-plow rating

Transmission: 1f-1r

Top speed: 2.0 mph

Weight: 6,000 lb.

1920 International Mogul 8-16

1916 International Harvester Titan 10-20

1919 International Harvester Mogul 10-20

Titan 10-20

Engine: 2-cylinder, horizontal, transverse, overhead valve

Bore and stroke: 6.50×8.00 in.

Displacement: 531 ci., kerosene fuel

Power: 13 drawbar hp, 28 belt hp; 3-plow rating

Transmission: 2f-1r

Top speed: 2.9 mph

Weight: 5,700 lb.

NTTL# 23

VARIATIONS

Mogul 8-16 (1914–1917), Mogul 10-20 (1916–1917), Titan 10-20 (1915–1922)

INTERNATIONAL HARVESTER
8-16 JUNIOR

A marked departure from previous tractors, the International 8-16 Junior was based on the then-current IH trucks. A four-cylinder truck engine and three-speed transmission were used. Unusual for the time for either trucks or tractors, the fan-cooled radiator was mounted behind the engine, above the flywheel. This had been done previously for military vehicles to protect the radiator from battle damage. Because this arrangement did not lend itself to a flat belt pulley, the 8-16 Junior became the first American tractor to have a rear PTO.

SPECIFICATIONS

8-16 Junior

Engine: 4-cylinder, vertical, inline, overhead valve

Bore and stroke: 4.25×5.00 in.

Displacement: 284 ci., kerosene fuel

Power: 11 drawbar hp, 19 belt hp; 2-plow rating

Transmission: 3f-1r

Top speed: 4.0 mph

Weight: 3,660 lb.

NTTL# 25

VARIATIONS

International 8-16 (1916–1922)

1919 International Harvester 8-16

INTERNATIONAL HARVESTER
MCCORMICK-DEERING 15-30, 10-20, AND 22-36

Conflict with the government over dual McCormick and Deering dealerships caused International Harvester to combine its dealers and make a new tractor, labeled McCormick-Deering. The McCormick-Deering 15-30 came out in 1921. It featured an engine with ball-bearing mains, an all-gear drive, and a unit frame. The seat and steering wheel were offset to the right to enhance plowing visibility, and the 15-30 had a foot-operated clutch and rear power take-off. The 15-30 replaced Mogul and Titan models.

Late in 1922, Harvester introduced a smaller, lighter, and cheaper tractor, the 10-20. It looked like the 15-30, but it was 2,000 pounds lighter and 14 inches shorter. Like the 15-30, it had a three-speed transmission, and the 284-cubic-inch engine had the same type of ball-bearing mains as the 15-30. It was available in narrow, orchard, and industrial versions. The 22-36, an upgrade of the 15-30, had a quarter-inch-larger bore and 50-rpm-higher operating speed.

1920s McCormick-Deering 10-20

SPECIFICATIONS

15-30

Engine: 4-cylinder, vertical, inline, overhead valve

Bore and stroke: 4.50×6.00 in.

Displacement: 382 ci., kerosene fuel

Power: 26 drawbar hp, 35 belt hp; 3-plow rating

Transmission: 2f-1r

Top speed: 4.0 mph

Weight: 6,000 lb.

NTTL# 130

10-20

Engine: 4-cylinder, vertical, inline, overhead valve

Bore and stroke: 4.25×5.00 in.

Displacement: 284 ci., kerosene fuel

Power: 16 drawbar hp, 25 belt hp; 2-plow rating

Transmission: 3f-1r

Top speed: 4.2 mph

Weight: 4,000 lb.

NTTL# 95

VARIATIONS

15-30 (1921–1928), 10-20 (1923–1939), 10-20 Industrial (1923–1940), 15-30 Industrial (1930–1932), 22-36 (1929–1934)

1928 Farmall Regular

INTERNATIONAL HARVESTER
FARMALL REGULAR, F-20, H, 300, AND 350

Tractors prior to 1924 were tailored for plowing and belt work. The rest of the farmer's daily tasks were not yet addressed by mechanization. Several implement makers, including Harvester, had looked into the possibility of engine-driven mowers, rakes, and cultivators, but nothing came of their experiments. The experimental department at IH worked on a motor cultivator from 1915 to 1918, and this experience was used to develop the first successful all-purpose farm tractor: the Farmall.

The first Farmalls were sold in 1924, although they could have been called field test models, since IH field men closely watched them. Production in earnest started in 1925. The new Farmall was capable of the draft and belt work of its predecessors, plus it had rear PTO output for powering harvesters and crop clearance for cultivating. Thus the Farmall could replace all the horses on the farm.

In 1932, the Farmall became a series of two models, the modernized F-20 and the larger F-30. To differentiate between the first Farmalls and the F-20 versions, the first

SPECIFICATIONS

McCormick-Deering Farmall (Regular)

Engine: 4-cylinder, vertical, inline, overhead valve

Bore and stroke: 3.75×5.00 in.

Displacement: 220 ci., kerosene fuel

Power: 13 drawbar hp, 20 belt hp; 2-plow rating

Transmission: 3f-1r

Top speed: 4.2 mph

Weight: 4,100 lb.

NTTL# 117

ABOVE 1939 Farmall F-20
OPPOSITE TOP 1942 Farmall H
OPPOSITE BOTTOM 1956 Farmall 300

picked up the nickname "Farmall Regular." There was also a golf-course version called the Fairway instead of Farmall. In 1937, the livery was changed from gray to red. Early Farmalls had cable-operated brakes linked to the steering. Brake pedals replaced the cables in 1939.

Later that year, the completely updated Farmall H appeared, styled by famous industrial designer Raymond Loewy. It had a more powerful engine, with 153 cubic inches. The H was produced until 1952, when it became the Super H, with 164 cubic inches. The Super H in turn became the 300 in 1954 (169 cubic inches) and 350 in 1956, the diesel with 193 cubic inches.

All variations of the Farmall series used four-cylinder overhead-valve engines. The H received a five-speed transmission, the Super H got hydraulics, and the 300 had an optional Torque Amplifier power shift half-step auxiliary. Gasoline, LPG, and diesel versions of the 350 were available. Continental made the 350's diesel engine.

International Harvester Farmall H

Engine: 4-cylinder, vertical, inline, overhead valve

Bore and stroke: 3.38×4.25 in.

Displacement: 153 ci., gasoline fuel

Power: 20 drawbar hp, 24 belt hp; 2-plow rating

Transmission: 5f-1r

Top speed: 16 mph

Weight: 3,875 lb.

NTTL# 333

VARIATIONS

Regular (1924–1931), Regular and Fairway (1926–1931), F-20 (1932–1939), H (1939–1952), Super H (1952–1954), 300 (1954–1956), 350 (1956–1958)

1938 Farmall F-30

INTERNATIONAL HARVESTER
FARMALL F-30, M, SUPER M, 400, AND 450

The F-30 Farmall went into production in late 1931. Its engine was basically the same as that of the 10-20, but it operated at a higher rpm. Battleship gray paint was used until November 1936, when the paint was changed to red. There were almost no changes to the basic design of the F-30 over its eight years of production.

The Farmall M, an all-new tractor with Raymond Loewy styling, replaced the F-30 in 1939. Conventional brake pedals that could be locked together replaced the cable-operated steering brakes. A new five-speed transmission gave added flexibility. Kerosene and gasoline versions were available, as was a diesel version, or MD. The M and MD engine blocks were the same except that the diesel had five, rather than three, main bearings. Starting was accomplished on gasoline with spark ignition. When the engine was warm, a lever was thrown, increasing the compression ratio, shutting off the carburetor, and engaging the diesel injectors.

SPECIFICATIONS

Farmall F-30

Engine: 4-cylinder, vertical, inline, overhead valve

Bore and stroke: 4.25×5.00 in.

Displacement: 284 ci., kerosene fuel

Power: 25 drawbar hp, 33 belt hp; 3-plow rating

Transmission: 4f-1r

Top speed: 3.8 mph

Weight: 5,900 lb.

NTTL# 198

The Super M (1952) was the same tractor as the M, but with an engine displacement increase to 264 cubic inches from 248. Hydraulics became standard equipment. An LPG option was available and a live hydraulic system added.

After two years, the Farmall 400 replaced the Super M. It could be ordered with a gasoline, diesel, or LPG engine. The engine was the same 264-cubic-inch unit offered on the Super M. The same five-speed transmission with Torque Amplifier was also continued. The Farmall "Fast Hitch" (an IH competitor to the three-point hitch) with Hydra-Touch hydraulics completed the picture, with a traction control feature added in 1956.

The Farmall 450 was a cosmetic update of the 400, except for an increase in engine displacement from 264 to 281 cubic inches. This put the 450 in the 50-horsepower class.

1957 Farmall 450

Engine: 4-cylinder, vertical, inline, overhead valve

Bore and stroke: 4.13×5.25 in.

Displacement: 281 ci., diesel fuel

Power: 35 drawbar hp, 49 belt hp; 4-plow rating

Transmission: 10f-1r

Top speed: 16 mph

Weight: 6,180 lb.

NTTL# 608

VARIATIONS

F-30 (1931–1939), M (1939–1952), Super M (1952–1954), Super MTA (1954), 400 (1954–1956), 450 (1956–1958)

TOP LEFT 1957 Farmall 450

BOTTOM LEFT 1954 International Harvester McCormick Deering Farmall Super M-LPG

INTERNATIONAL HARVESTER
W-4 SERIES, 300, 330, 340, AND 350 UTILITIES

The W-4 was a standard-tread version of the Farmall H row crop tractor, but a four-speed transmission was used. Orchard and grove variations, labeled OS-4 and O-4, were the same, except that the O-4 had streamlined rear fenders and relocated lights, air intake, and exhaust pipe. The Super W-4 replaced the W-4 in the lineup in 1953, with a 164-cubic-inch engine, five-speed transmission, and modifications to the grille and front frame.

The 300 Utility replaced it the following year. The 300 Utility was the standard-tread version of the Farmall 300 row crop. The engine was rated at a higher speed, however, giving the 300 Utility slightly more horsepower. It was available with an LPG engine.

In the same way, the International 350 Utility corresponded to the Farmall 350 row crop. It too was available in gasoline, LPG, or Continental-built diesel. The International 330 Utility did not have a corresponding row crop tractor. It used the 135-cubic-inch engine. The International 340 (utility) and Farmall 340 (row crop) also used the 135-cubic-inch engine. Both the 330 and 340 were available with the Torque Amplifier transmission, to go with their regular five-speed units. All could be equipped with either the Fast Hitch or three-point hitch.

SPECIFICATIONS

W-4

Engine: 4-cylinder, vertical, inline, overhead valve

Bore and stroke: 3.38×4.25 in.

Displacement: 153 ci., gasoline fuel

Power: 21 drawbar hp, 24 belt hp; 2-plow rating

Transmission: 4f-1r

Top speed: 5 mph

Weight: 3,816 lb.

NTTL# 342

300 Utility

Engine: 4-cylinder, vertical, inline, overhead valve

Bore and stroke: 3.56×4.25 in.

Displacement: 169 ci., gasoline fuel

Power: 30 drawbar hp, 39 belt hp; 3-plow rating

Transmission: 10f-1r

Top speed: 16 mph

Weight: 4,413 lb.

NTTL# 539

VARIATIONS

W-4, O-4, OS-4 (all 1940–1953), Super W-4 (1953–1954), 300 Utility (1955–1956), 350 Utility (1957–1958), 330 (1957–1958), 340 (1958–1963)

ABOVE 1955 International Harvester 300 Utility

TOP 1951 International Harvester W-4

INTERNATIONAL HARVESTER
W-30, W-6
SERIES, W-400,
AND W-450

Starting in 1932, IH offered the McCormick-Deering W-30, a standard-tread version of the F-30 Farmall. The W-30 used the same roller-bearing engine, but an increase in rated speed and compression ratio gave more power. Orchard and industrial versions were offered. The W-30 kept the three-speed transmission when the F-30 went to four. (IH also made a 30, an industrial tractor that was a derivation of the 15-30 and not related to the W-30.)

The W-6 had the same engine and transmission as the Farmall M. The same was true of the Super W-6 and Farmall Super M, including their gasoline, diesel, and LPG fuel versions and Torque Amplifier auxiliary transmission. O-6 and OS-6 orchard tractors were also available with the same engines and transmissions.

1938 International Harvester McCormick-Deering W-30

SPECIFICATIONS

W-30

Engine: 4-cylinder, vertical, inline, overhead valve

Bore and stroke: 4.25×5.00 in.

Displacement: 284 ci., kerosene fuel

Power: 20 drawbar hp, 33 belt hp; 3-plow rating

Transmission: 4f-1r

Top speed: 3.8 mph

Weight: 5,575 lb.

NTTL# 210

W-400

Engine: 4-cylinder, vertical, inline, overhead valve

Bore and stroke: 4.00×5.25 in.

Displacement: 264 ci., gasoline fuel

Power: 38 drawbar hp, 49 belt hp; 4-plow rating

Transmission: 10f-1r

Top speed: 16 mph

Weight: 6,328 lb.

NTTL# 533

1956 International Harvester W-400 Diesel

The W-400 paralleled the Farmall 400. Diesel, LPG, and gasoline versions were offered, as was the Torque Amplifier. The same relationship existed for the W-450 and Farmall 450. Only about 4,000 W-450s of all fuel types were made.

VARIATIONS

W-30, I-30 (both 1932–1940), W-6, O-6, OS-6 (all 1940–1953), Super W-6 (1952–1954), W-400 (1955–1956), W-450 (1956–1958)

1939 International Harvester McCormick Deering W-40

INTERNATIONAL HARVESTER
W-40, WD-40, W-9, 600, 650, AND 660

The first of the big McCormick-Deering wheatland standard-treads was the W-40, which came out in 1934 and featured a six-cylinder engine of the type used in IH heavy-duty trucks. It was available in either 279-cubic-inch (gasoline) or 298-cubic-inch (distillate fuel) versions. According to Nebraska tests 268 and 269 (see page 7), two rated speeds were available: 1,600 rpm or 1,750 rpm.

The WD-40 was the same tractor but with a four-cylinder diesel engine of 471 cubic inches. It was the first diesel wheeled tractor. Both the W-40 and WD-40 were available as industrial tractors.

The McCormick W-9 replaced the W-40 in 1940. It featured stylish Raymond Loewy–designed sheet metal and a 335-cubic-inch four-cylinder engine of the type used in the International Harvester T-9 crawler, with a five-speed transmission. The diesel-powered WD-9, introduced in 1945, had basically the same engine, beefed up to handle diesel loads.

The 600 was essentially the same as the WD-9, as was the 650. The 660, however, was considerably different and completely restyled. The Torque Amplifier was added. The engines were six-cylinder types, 281 cubic inches for diesel and 263 cubic inches for gasoline and LPG versions. These were high-speed engines operating at 2,400 rpm and producing about 80 horsepower.

SPECIFICATIONS
WD-40

Engine: 4-cylinder, vertical, inline, overhead valve

Bore and stroke: 4.75×6.50 in.

Displacement: 471 ci., diesel fuel

Power: 35 drawbar hp, 49 belt hp; 4-plow rating

Transmission: 3f-1r

Top speed: 3.9 mph

Weight: 8,450 lb.

NTTL# 246

VARIATIONS

W-40 andWD-40 (both 1934–1940), W-9 (1940–1953), WD-9 (1945–1953), Super WD-9 (1953–1956), 600 (1956), 650 (1956–1958), 660 (1959–1963)

1941 Farmall A

INTERNATIONAL HARVESTER
FARMALL A, B, C, 100, 200, AND 240

The Farmall A, which came out in 1939, was the first of the letter-series tractors from International Harvester. The A was also the first "offset" tractor, with the engine and drivetrain offset to the left and driver and steering wheel to the right, giving the driver an unobstructed view of the cultivator shovels mounted beneath the tractor.

Models A and B were mechanically the same, but the A had a wide front end. It used one long axle in the back on the right and one short one on the left. The B had a tricycle front and used two long rear axles. As with other Farmalls, the 1952 upgraded version of the A was called the Super A.

The Farmall C replaced the B in 1948. It was the same mechanically as the B, but now it had an operator's platform; it stood higher and looked larger. It also offered optional hydraulics. A Super C came out in 1952.

The Farmall 100, 130, and 140 were upgraded and restyled versions of the original A. Likewise, the 200 and 230 were improved models of the C. The 240 was a complete redesign. Gone was the platform. Instead, the operator sat forward, straddling the transmission.

SPECIFICATIONS
Farmall A

Engine: 4-cylinder, vertical, inline, overhead valve

Bore and stroke: 3.00×4.00 in.

Displacement: 113 ci., gasoline fuel

Power: 12 drawbar hp, 17 belt hp; 1-plow rating

Transmission: 4f-1r

Top speed: 10 mph

Weight: 2,014 lb.

NTTL# 329

VARIATIONS

A (1939–1952), B (1939–1947), C (1948–1951), Super A (1952–1954), Super C (1952–1954), 100 (1954–1956), 130 (1956–1958), 140 (1958–1979), 200 (1954–1956), 230 (1956–1958), 240 (1958–1962)

INTERNATIONAL HARVESTER
F-12 AND F-14 SERIES

The diminutive Farmall F-12 made its debut in late 1932. Only about 550 were made that year, equipped with a Waukesha engine. This was soon replaced by a 113-cubic-inch four-cylinder overhead-valve engine of Harvester's own design. The tractor was like a scale model of the F-20 and F-30, but rather than a drop box final drive, the F-12 used straight splined axles so that infinite rear-wheel spacing could be accomplished. At first, a single front wheel was used, but soon dual-tricycle and wide fronts were available. Also available were a central rear PTO, rubber tires, and a mechanical implement lift. Gasoline fuel was standard, but a kerosene manifold and starting gas tank were extra-cost options.

SPECIFICATIONS
Farmall F-12

Engine: 4-cylinder, vertical, inline, overhead valve

Bore and stroke: 3.00×4.00 in.

Displacement: 113 ci., gasoline fuel

Power: 12 drawbar hp, 16 belt hp; 1-plow rating

Transmission: 3f-1r

Top speed: 4 mph

Weight: 3,360 lb.

NTTL# 212

1936 Farmall F-12

The standard-tread version of the F-12 was the W-12. It was the same mechanically, but it was built lower and with fixed tread widths. Additional variations of the W-12 configuration emerged: O-12 (orchard), I-12 (industrial), and fairway models for golf courses and airports, with special use–oriented wheels and tires. Only about six hundred Fairway 12s were sold.

More than 123,000 F-12s had been delivered by the time production ended. The almost-identical Model F-14 replaced the F-12 in 1938, the only visible difference being that the steering wheel and shaft were raised to a more comfortable angle and position. Increasing the engine speed from 1,400 to 1,650 rpm provided about 14 percent more horsepower, enough to give the F-14 a two-plow rating. It was available in gasoline and kerosene versions, and on steel or rubber tires. Wheel weights were an option when rubber tires were specified. A hydraulic implement lift was another option. W-14, I-14, O-14, and Fairway 14 versions were similar to those of the 12 series. Electric starting and lights were available for the W-14 and O-14. Interestingly, the 12 and 14 series tractors were the only ones made at the time by IH that used fuel pumps.

Farmall F-14

Engine: 4-cylinder, vertical, inline, overhead valve

Bore and stroke: 3.00×4.00 in.

Displacement: 113 ci., distillate fuel

Power: 13 drawbar hp, 17 belt hp; 2-plow rating

Transmission: 3f-1r

Top speed: 5 mph

Weight: 3,614 lb.

NTTL# 297

VARIATIONS

F-12 (1933–1938), W-12 (1932–1940), Fairway 12 (1934–1938), I-12 (1934–1938), O-12 (1935–1938), F-14 (1938–1939), W-14 (1938–1939), Fairway 14 (1938–1939), I-14 (1939)

1939 Farmall F-14

INTERNATIONAL HARVESTER
FARMALL
CUB AND
INTERNATIONAL
CUB

Since A and B designators had already been used, and higher letters indicated larger tractors in the Farmall lineup, the naming committee was stuck—until they came up with the "Cub" name. Small, friendly, and cute: the name conjured all those adjectives. The configuration of the Cub was virtually identical to the Farmall A, and unless seen together, they were difficult to tell apart. Features of the Cub included a rear PTO with or without a belt pulley, steering brakes, and, later, a hydraulic implement lift, starter, and lights. A special low-slung version for mowing was called the Cub Lo-Boy.

The Cub retained a three-speed transmission throughout its life. The Farmall name was dropped in 1958, although some Cub Lo-Boys were labeled "Farmall" into 1964. Most Cub Lo-Boys were International Harvesters (rather than Farmalls), as were regular Cubs after 1958. Production of International Cubs continued through 1975. Like the rest of the IH tractor line, the Cub received styling and paint changes over the course of its lifetime.

SPECIFICATIONS

Farmall Cub

Engine: 4-cylinder, vertical, inline, side valve

Bore and stroke: 2.63×2.75 in.

Displacement: 60 ci., gasoline fuel

Power: 8 drawbar hp, 10 belt hp; 1-plow rating

Transmission: 3f-1r

Top speed: 6 mph

Weight: 1,477 lb.

NTTL# 386

VARIATIONS

Cub (1947–1958), Lo-Boy (1955–1975), International Cub (1958–1975)

1949 Farmall Cub

INTERNATIONAL HARVESTER
FARMALL 460 AND 560

The 460, introduced in 1958, was a 50-horsepower tractor, rated for four plow bottoms and available in gasoline, diesel, or LPG versions. It also came in dual narrow-front, adjustable wide-front, or high-clearance wide-front configurations.

The diesel version featured the D-236 six-cylinder IH engine, with glow plug starting. The gasoline and LPG engines were C-221 sixes. The numerical engine designator indicated the displacement in cubic inches; "C" or "D" indicated a spark ignition or diesel type, respectively.

Besides bold new styling, the 460 featured an internal hydraulic pump, an instrument panel, a seat with a backrest, and a 12-volt electrical system (albeit with a generator rather than an alternator). The five-speed transmission with Torque Amplifier was standard. New for the 460—replacing over-the-engine steering—was a steering shaft assembly (with universal joints) that ran down from the instrument panel to the frame, then forward to a steering gearbox. Power steering was standard.

The Farmall 560 also came out in 1958 as the big brother of the 460. It was a five-plow tractor in the 60-horsepower class, and it was the top of the IH row crop line of tractors, supplanting the Farmall 450. All-new styling featured a long, powerful hood covering a smooth-running six-cylinder engine. The 560 had a seat with a backrest, a 12-volt electrical system (with a generator rather than an alternator), an internal hydraulic pump, and an instrument panel. Gasoline, LPG, and diesel versions were available, the latter featuring the D-282 six-cylinder IH engine. The gasoline and LPG engines were C-263 sixes. As in the 460, the five-speed transmission with Torque Amplifier was standard. The 560 had a steering system like that of the 460, with power steering standard.

SPECIFICATIONS
Farmall 460

Engine: 6-cylinder, vertical, inline, overhead valve

Bore and stroke: 3.69×3.69 in.

Displacement: 236 ci., diesel fuel

Power: 37 drawbar hp, 50 PTO hp; 4-plow rating

Transmission: 10f-2r

Top speed: 17 mph

Weight: 5,485 lb.

NTTL# 672

Farmall 560

Engine: 6-cylinder, vertical, inline, overhead valve

Bore and stroke: 3.69×4.39 in.

Displacement: 282 ci., diesel fuel

Power: 45 drawbar hp, 59 PTO hp; 5-plow rating

Transmission: 10f-2r

Top speed: 16 mph

Weight: 6,172 lb.

NTTL# 672

VARIATIONS

Farmall 460 and 560 (1958–1963)

ABOVE 1959 Farmall 560 Diesel

TOP 1962 Farmall 460

Massey-Harris

Racine, Wisconsin, and Toronto, Ontario

In 1891, two Canadian farm equipment giants formed Massey-Harris: the Massey Manufacturing Company of Toronto and A. Harris, Son & Company Ltd. of Brantford. Both companies had beginnings before the middle of the nineteenth century, and each grew stronger battling the other for patents for new types of harvesting equipment. By the late 1880s, they were numbers one and two in the Canadian farm equipment market. It was at that time that the companies' managers realized that further competition could be ruinous, and together, they could successfully compete with John Deere and International Harvester in the North American marketplace.

1917 Massey-Harris Big Bull

BULL, NO. 1, 2, AND 3

Because they did not want to hurt their sale of tractor-drawn equipment by competing in tractors, Massey-Harris did not add a proprietary tractor to their product line until 1917. Instead, their first venture was in 1916 with the Bull Tractor, sold under license. The Bull, originated by the Minneapolis Steel & Machinery Company, was a phenomenon that originally had hit the market in 1913 with much ballyhoo and a $335 price tag.

The Bull used a two-cylinder engine acquired from the Toro Motor Company, also of Minneapolis. The Bull's performance in the field was less than satisfactory, and the arrangement with M-H only lasted a year.

SPECIFICATIONS

Big Bull

Engine: 2-cylinder, horizontally opposed, side valve

Bore and stroke: 5.50×7.00 in.

Displacement: 333 ci., kerosene fuel

Power: 12 drawbar hp, 25 belt hp; 1-plow rating

Transmission: 1f-1r

Top speed: 2.4 mph

Weight: 4,870 lb.

1923 Massey-Harris No. 3

When the Bull deal fell through, Massey-Harris opted to build an American tractor designed by the Parrett brothers—pioneer tractor designers and manufacturers from Chicago—under license in their factory in Weston, Ontario. It had large front wheels, automotive-type steering, and open final drive gears. This, the Massey-Harris No. 1, used a Buda engine. An improved version, No. 2 (1920), had shielding to keep dirt out of the final drive gears. A guide for the flat belt was added to keep the belt from jumping off its pulley. The Massey-Harris No. 3 (1922) had a larger Buda engine and a transverse radiator, giving the tractor a more contemporary appearance.

Massey-Harris No. 3

Engine: 4-cylinder, vertical, transverse, overhead valve

Bore and stroke: 4.50×6.25 in.

Displacement: 398 ci., kerosene fuel

Power: 15 drawbar hp, 28 belt hp; 2-plow rating

Transmission: 2f-1r

Top speed: 3.3 mph

Weight: 5,800 lb.

VARIATIONS

Bull (1917), Massey-Harris No. 1, 2, and 3 (1920–1923)

1958 Massey-Harris 25

MASSEY-HARRIS
20-30, 25, AND 12

Massey-Harris purchased J. I. Case Plow Works in 1928, at the time managed by Henry Wallis. Wallis had previously sold his Wallis Tractor Company, producing a Wallis-brand line of tractors, to Case. Under Massey-Harris, production of the Wallis Model 20-30 continued. The tractor featured a U-shaped boilerplate frame, which also served as the crankcase of the engine. Wallis had pioneered this construction, wherein the rear-axle housing, transmission, and engine structure replaced a conventional frame—a concept that came to be known as the "unit frame concept."

The 20-30 used a four-cylinder engine and two-speed transmission. It had a hand brake, governor, and optional lights. The tractor was revamped in 1931 and called the Massey-Harris Model 25, with an increase in engine rpm and a three-speed transmission. A "styled" version came out in 1938.

SPECIFICATIONS
25

Engine: 4-cylinder, vertical, inline, overhead valve

Bore and stroke: 4.38×5.75 in.

Displacement: 347 ci., kerosene fuel

Power: 35 drawbar hp, 48 belt hp; 4-plow rating

Transmission: 3f-1r

Top speed: 3.3 mph

Weight: 4,919 lb.

NTTL# 219

1936 Massey-Harris Twin Power Pacemaker

The Wallis-Certified Model 12-20 (1932), a scaled-down version of the Model 25, was built to fill the need for a two-plow machine. It was called the Model 12 but was subsequently named the Pacemaker. A row crop version was called the Challenger. In 1937, the Pacemaker and Challenger received styled sheet metal, upgraded engines, and the Massey-exclusive "Twin Power" feature. With Twin Power, the engine rpm could be increased for belt and PTO work. Regular engine speed and horsepower were available for work through the transmission and drivetrain.

Twin Power Pacemaker

Engine: 4-cylinder, vertical, inline, overhead valve

Bore and stroke: 3.38×5.25 in.

Displacement: 248 ci., gasoline fuel

Power: 20 drawbar hp, 42 belt hp; 2-plow rating

Transmission: 4f-1r

Top speed: 8.5 mph

Weight: 3,755 lb.

NTTL# 294

VARIATIONS

20-30 Model 25 (1926–1941), 12-20 Model 12 (1929–1935), Pacemaker Model PA (1936–1937), Challenger Model CH (1936–1937), Pacemaker (Styled) (1937–1939), Challenger (Styled) (1937–1939

MASSEY-HARRIS
GP FOUR-WHEEL DRIVE

The GP Four-Wheel Drive, the first tractor developed by Massey-Harris engineers and the first for the Racine operation that came with the acquisition of Case Plow Works, was a giant step taken in an effort not only to catch up, but to jump ahead of the competition. All four equal-sized wheels were powered through a transfer case and differentials on each axle. The front axle had a universal-joint steering arrangement for front wheels, each of which had an independent brake. The rear axle was free in the roll axis, allowing all four wheels to remain in contact with uneven ground. A Hercules four-cylinder engine gave the 4,000-pound tractor a 15/22 rating. A three-speed gearbox was provided, as were a belt pulley and rear PTO. Crop clearance under the axles was 30 inches.

The GP had optional starter and lights and an implement lift. The tractor was available in four different widths for different row spacing, although not adjustable. Orchard, railroad, golf-course, and industrial models, some with rubber tires, were also available. In 1936, an improved version with an overhead-valve four was introduced, identified by a hood slanted slightly downward toward the front.

SPECIFICATIONS
GP Four-Wheel Drive

Engine: 4-cylinder, vertical, inline, side valve

Bore and stroke: 4.00×4.50 in.

Displacement: 226 ci., gasoline fuel

Power: 16 drawbar hp, 25 belt hp; 2-plow rating

Transmission: 3f-1r

Top speed: 4.0 mph

Weight: 3,861 lb.

NTTL# 177

VARIATIONS

GP (side valve) (1930–1936), GP (overhead valve) (1936–1938)

1930 Massey-Harris GP Four-Wheel Drive

MASSEY-HARRIS
GENERAL GG

Competition in the small, inexpensive tractor market was such that in 1939, Massey-Harris, who had nothing to offer their customers, made a deal with the Cleveland Tractor Company (Cletrac) of Cleveland, Ohio, to sell Cletrac's small and simple $600 "General GG" in Canada. These were identical to those sold by Cletrac in the United States, even down to the orange paint. But the serial-number tag stated that the tractor was built for Massey-Harris. A Hercules four-cylinder engine powered it. Massey sold the General in small numbers through 1942, when the Massey-Harris Model 81 replaced it.

The General was also sold in the United States by Montgomery Ward, as the Wards Twin Row. Cletrac eventually sold the design of the General to the B. F. Avery & Company of Louisville, Kentucky, which was then taken over by Minneapolis-Moline. Minneapolis-Moline sold the little tractor as their Model BF.

SPECIFICATIONS
General GG

Engine: 4-cylinder, vertical, inline, side valve

Bore and stroke: 3.00×4.00 in.

Displacement: 113 ci., gasoline fuel

Power: 12 drawbar hp, 18 belt hp; 1-plow rating

Transmission: 3f-1r

Top speed: 6.0 mph

Weight: 2,105 lb.

VARIATIONS
General GG (1939–1942)

1941 Massey-Harris Cletrac General GG

MODELS 101 JUNIOR, 81, 20, 22, 21 COLT, AND 23 MUSTANG

Massey's first smaller tractor came out in 1939 as the Model 101 Junior. A Continental four-cylinder side-valve engine was used, originally with 124-cubic-inch displacement, soon increased to 140 cubic inches. In 1943, a 162-cubic-inch version replaced it. All sizes used the same engine, with the bore being increased. The tractor was available in both standard-tread and row crop models. Both gasoline (101 Junior) and distillate (102 Junior) versions were available; however, as distillate's favor waned, the 102 Junior designation was reapplied to tractors destined for overseas shipment. The tractor featured Twin Power (see page 116), with a drawbar-rated speed of 1,500 rpm and 1,800 rpm reserved for belt work and fourth gear. Fenders were standard. Also included in the base price were individual brakes, a belt pulley, a PTO, an electrical system with a starter, and a swinging drawbar. Optional equipment included a power implement lift system.

SPECIFICATIONS

101 Junior

Engine: 4-cylinder, vertical, inline, side valve

Bore and stroke: 3.19×4.38 in.

Displacement: 140 ci., gasoline fuel

Power: 19 drawbar hp, 30 belt hp; 2-plow rating

Transmission: 4f-1r

Top speed: 17.0 mph

Weight: 3,250 lb.

NTTL# 359

1941 Massey-Harris 101 Junior

1953 Massey-Harris 23 Mustang

The Model 81 was another approach to making small farm tractors. It was intended to replace the Model GG General, with an in-house design. The 81 and 82, its distillate-burning counterpart, were much the same as the Model 101/102 Junior, although the price was somewhat lower. The 81 and 82 were available in row crop or standard tread and featured Twin Power. The 81 used the 124-cubic-inch engine; the 82 used the 140-cubic-inch unit.

A Model 20 debuted in 1947 as part of a new line of tractors celebrating Massey-Harris's one-hundredth anniversary. It was virtually the same as the old Model 81/82, and it was replaced in 1948 by the Model 22, which used the 140-cubic-inch Continental engine and offered hydraulics and a three-point lift.

The Model 21 Colt replaced the Model 20/22, with new styling and a starter and lights, thermostat, oil pressure gage, ammeter, and fenders as standard equipment. Options included a three-point hitch, deluxe seat, tachometer/hour meter, and belt pulley. The Model 23 Mustang offered the same styling and modernizations but with a larger engine.

23 Mustang

Engine: 4-cylinder, vertical, inline, side valve

Bore and stroke: 3.19×4.38 in.

Displacement: 140 ci., gasoline fuel

Power: 23 drawbar hp, 31 belt hp; 2-plow rating

Transmission: 4f-1r

Top speed: 14.0 mph

Weight: 2,785 lb.

VARIATIONS

101/102 Jr. (1939–1946), 81/82 (1941–1946), 20 (1947–1948), 22 (1948–1953), 21 Colt (1952–1953), 23 Mustang (1952–1956)

MASSEY-HARRIS
MODELS 11 PONY, 14 PONY, AND 16 PACER

The 11 Pony was built in the Woodstock, Ontario, Canada, plant, 90 miles southwest of Toronto. It used a tiny four-cylinder Continental side-valve engine, but it was a serious machine built for heavy and continuous work.

In 1954 and 1955, some Ponys were painted gray and distributed through Ferguson dealers during the Two-Line Policy. Counting all variations, the Pony series was the most popular of all Massey-Harris tractors. The Model 14 Pony was the same as the 11, except for the inclusion of a fluid coupling between the engine and clutch. This device eliminated jerky starts and was aimed at towing jobs, especially moving aircraft. Only about seventy-five Model 14s were made.

The Model 16 Pacer was a Pony on steroids. It used a 91-cubic-inch Continental four-cylinder engine; it was longer and heavier and cost more than the Pony. It had an engine-driven hydraulic implement lift and a live PTO. The Pacer used the same three-speed transmission as the Pony.

There were also Pony tractors built in France from 1951 to 1961 in three versions: Models 811, 812, and 820. The same chassis was used but with engines from Simca and Hanomag (diesel).

SPECIFICATIONS
11 Pony

Engine: 4-cylinder, vertical, inline, side valve

Bore and stroke: 2.38×3.50 in.

Displacement: 62 ci., gasoline fuel

Power: 11 drawbar hp, 12 belt hp; 1-plow rating

Transmission: 3f-1r

Top speed: 7 mph

Weight: 1,365 lb.

NTTL# 401

VARIATIONS

Model 11 Pony (1947–1957), Model 14 Pony (1951–1953), Model 16 Pacer (1953–1955)

1948 Massey-Harris 11 Pony

MASSEY-HARRIS
MODELS 30, 33,
AND 333

The Model 30 replaced the 101 Junior in 1947. It was updated and restyled, and although it retained the four-cylinder 162-cubic-inch Continental engine of the Junior, it was an all-new tractor. New for the Model 30 was a five-speed transmission. It was available with either gasoline or distillate fuel systems. Engine paint changed from black to red in 1948.

The Massey-Harris Model 33 succeeded the 30 in late 1952 as a 1953 model, available in row crop and standard-tread versions. A four-cylinder Continental-built engine replaced the 30's side-valve unit, and the Twin Power concept was dropped. Gasoline, distillate, and diesels were used. Hydraulics and the three-point "Lift-All" hitch were optional, as was a live PTO.

SPECIFICATIONS

30

Engine: 4-cylinder, vertical, inline, side valve

Bore and stroke: 3.44×4.38 in.

Displacement: 162 ci., gasoline fuel

Power: 26 drawbar hp, 34 belt hp; 3-plow rating

Transmission: 5f-1r

Top speed: 13.0 mph

Weight: 3,475 lb.

NTTL# 409

1948 Massey-Harris 30

1956 Massey-Harris 333

For the 1956 model year, the Massey-Harris Model 333 replaced the Model 33, with a new bronze engine color scheme and with some chrome trim added to the grille. The bore increased, and a 12-volt electrical system was adopted, although generators, rather than the later alternators, continued to be used into the 1960s. Also new was a two-range power shift, giving a total of ten speeds forward and two in reverse. In addition to the standard gasoline, other offered versions were distillate, diesel, and LPG. A version of Ferguson's draft-control three-point hitch was an option, as were power steering and a choice of front-end arrangements, which included single front wheel, dual-tricycle, and an adjustable-width utility axle. A standard-tread version was available but rare.

333

Engine: 4-cylinder, vertical, inline, overhead valve

Bore and stroke: 3.69×4.88 in.

Displacement: 208 ci., gasoline fuel

Power: 30 drawbar hp, 44 belt hp; 3-plow rating

Transmission: 10f-2r

Top speed: 14.0 mph

Weight: 5,920 lb.

NTTL# 603

VARIATIONS

30 (1947–1952), 33 (1952–1955), 333 (1956–1957)

1938 Massey-Harris 101

MASSEY-HARRIS
MODELS 101, 101 SUPER, AND 101-102 SENIOR

The 101 debuted in 1938, inaugurating the great Massey-Harris series of tractors with Chrysler engines. The well-experienced, smooth-running, lightweight, side-valve, six-cylinder Chrysler engine would give the Oliver Farm Equipment Company some competition against its new six-cylinder 70. Chrysler engine parts and service were already available worldwide.

The 101, with its chrome striping and fully louvered hood side panels, was one of the world's most strikingly beautiful tractors of all time. The Chrysler engine purred with a mellow quietness. Since Chrysler products had had electric starters for years, one was included on the 101—a first as standard equipment for any major tractor manufacturer. The "Super" designation was added in 1939 to avoid confusion with the new 101 Junior (see page 119). In 1940, the engine size of the 101 Super increased from 201 to 217.7 cubic inches.

SPECIFICATIONS

101

Engine: 6-cylinder, vertical, inline, side valve

Bore and stroke: 3.13×4.38 in.

Displacement: 201 ci., gasoline fuel

Power: 31 drawbar hp, 40 belt hp; 3-plow rating

Transmission: 4f-1r

Top speed: 17.0 mph

Weight: 3,650 lb.

NTTL# 309

All Massey-Harris tractors in the 101/102 series employed the Twin Power feature. The drawbar engine speed was 1,500 rpm, and for belt work, the speed was 1,800 rpm. At the lower speed, the drivetrain would not be overtorqued. The 1,800-rpm engine speed was available only in neutral or fourth gear, giving a road speed of almost 20 miles per hour. These engine speeds were about half of the engine's rated rpm when used in a car or truck, but the tractor engine nevertheless proved to be gutsy, with good lugging torque.

In 1942, the 101 Senior replaced the 101 Super, with Twin Power retained and with a 226-cubic-inch six-cylinder Continental engine. A 244-cubic-inch version of the engine, configured for distillate fuel, powered the 102 Senior. As gasoline became the US fuel of choice, the 102 Senior designator was used for export tractors. The Twin Power feature was retained from the Super series; the fancy louvered side hoods were not. The Senior series was much the same as the Super, except for the engine change. A four-speed transmission was provided for both. The row crop versions had adjustable rear-wheel spacing and individual rear-wheel brakes. A power take-off and implement lift were optional. Senior tractors were not delivered to the University of Nebraska for testing (see page 7).

101 Senior

Engine: 6-cylinder, vertical, inline, side valve

Bore and stroke: 3.25×4.38 in.

Displacement: 226 ci., gasoline fuel

Power: 36 drawbar hp, 49 belt hp (est.); 3-plow rating

Transmission: 4f-1r

Top speed: 12.0 mph

Weight: 3,760 lb.

VARIATIONS

101 (1938), 101 Super (1939–1942), 101–102 Senior (1942–1946)

1942 Massey-Harris 101 Senior

MASSEY-HARRIS
MODELS 201, 202, AND 203

Massey management decided to build a big standard-tread plowing tractor for the western plains around a new Chrysler engine, with a displacement of 242 cubic inches. The result was the Model 201, some 500 of which were built. The engine's long stroke gave it great lugging torque. Twin Power was used, with 1,700-rpm drawbar speed and 2,000 rpm for road gear and belt work. A four-speed transmission was provided, as were left and right brakes that could be locked together when not contributing to steering. Not tested at the University of Nebraska, the 201 was considered to be a four-plow tractor.

The Massey-Harris Model 202, also introduced in 1940, was the same as the 201, except that it was equipped with a 290-cubic-inch Continental engine. Although not tested at the University of Nebraska, the 202 was labeled a five-plow tractor. Only 223 Model 202s were built. A Model 203 distillate version was offered starting in 1940, using a Continental engine of 330-cubic-inch displacement. In 1944, a Model 203G gasoline version was added. Almost 3,000 203s were built.

SPECIFICATIONS

201

Engine: 6-cylinder, vertical, inline, side valve

Bore and stroke: 3.38×4.50 in.

Displacement: 242 ci., gasoline fuel

Power: 37 drawbar hp, 48 belt hp; 4-plow rating

Transmission: 4f-1r

Top speed: 12.0 mph

Weight: 6,435 lb.

203

Engine: 6-cylinder, vertical, inline, side valve

Bore and stroke: 4.00×4.38 in.

Displacement: 330 ci., gasoline fuel

Power: 50 drawbar hp, 62 belt hp; 5-plow rating

Transmission: 4f-1r

Top speed: 13.0 mph

Weight: 6,600 lb.

VARIATIONS

201 (1940–1942), 202 (1940–1942), 203 (1940–1947)

1941 Massey-Harris 203

MODELS 44, 44-6, 744PD, 745, 44 SPECIAL, AND 444

The first of the postwar tractors from Massey-Harris was the standard-tread Model 44, which came out in 1946, with a row crop version appearing the following year. The Model 44 used a four-cylinder Continental engine with versions for gasoline, distillate, LPG, or diesel fuels (the diesel was added in 1948). Orchard, vineyard, and high-altitude configurations were available. For the company's one-hundredth anniversary, throughout the line, the 44 received new styling with more rounded contours. It was the first Massey tractor to have a live PTO. In 1950, a hydraulic lift was added.

The Model 44-6, six-cylinder, came out in 1947 in both row crop and standard-tread configurations. Because the Oliver Farm Equipment Company (see page 142) had touted the smoothness of the six-cylinder engine since 1935, one was offered in the new postwar lineup, the same 226-cubic-inch side-valve Continental used in the M-H 101 Senior. Otherwise, the 44-6 was the same as the

SPECIFICATIONS

44

Engine: 4-cylinder, vertical, inline, overhead valve

Bore and stroke: 3.88×5.50 in.

Displacement: 260 ci., gasoline fuel

Power: 40 drawbar hp, 46 belt hp; 3-plow rating

Transmission: 5f-1r

Top speed: 14.0 mph

Weight: 3,855 lb.

NTTL# 389

Massey-Harris 44

Model 44, but slightly longer, and it was only configured for gasoline fuel.

Starting in 1948, the Model 44 was also built in Great Britain, called the 744PD. A six-cylinder Perkins P6 diesel of 288 cubic inches, developing 46 horsepower, was used. A Model 745 came out in place of the 744PD in 1954. It was the same, except that a four-cylinder Perkins diesel was used in place of the six.

The Model 44 Special was a 1955 upgrade of the original 44. The displacement of the engine increased to 277 cubic inches, putting the power just under 50 horsepower. A five-speed gearbox, live PTO, and hydraulic three-point hitch were standard. Row crop, standard-tread, cane, and high crop versions were made. Those made for high altitude, for distillate or LPG fuels, reverted to the 260-cubic-inch engine.

The Model 444 came out in 1956. It had the same 277-cubic-inch engine as the 44 Special in gas, diesel, LPG, and distillate versions. A two-speed auxiliary power shift transmission, along with the standard five-speed, gave ten forward speeds and two in reverse. Power steering was an extra-cost option; a 12-volt electrical system was standard.

1956 Model 444

Engine: 4-cylinder, vertical, inline, overhead valve

Bore and stroke: 4.00×5.50 in.

Displacement: 277 ci., diesel fuel

Power: 46 drawbar hp, 51 belt hp; 4-plow rating

Transmission: 10f-2r

Top speed: 14.0 mph

Weight: 5,258 lb.

NTTL# 576

VARIATIONS

44 (1946–1953), 44-6 (1946–1951), 44 Special (1953–1955), 744PD (1948–1953), 745 (1954–1958), 444 (1956–1958)

1957 Massey-Harris 444

MASSEY-HARRIS
MODELS 50, 55,
AND 555

The Model 50 was hurriedly adapted from the Ferguson TO-35 immediately after the merger of the two companies and the instigation of the two-line dealership concept. It was an attempt to placate Massey-Harris dealers who had nothing like the TO-35 on offer to compete with Ferguson dealers. Besides Massey sheet metal and paint, the 50 differed in that it could be configured as either a utility or row crop. When Ferguson dealers saw what they were up against, they demanded the same thing. Thus, with Ferguson colors and styling, the same tractor (under the skin) became the Ferguson 40, and after the end of the two-line policy, it became the Massey Ferguson 50. All relied on the Nebraska tests of the TO-35.

The Massey-Harris Model 55 standard-tread tractor was introduced with the other two-number tractors at the end of 1946 for the 1947 centennial model year, a replacement for the 201, 202, and 203 series tractors. Continental built its new four-cylinder overhead-valve engine for Massey-Harris. It was rated at 1,350 rpm and did not have the Twin Power feature. Originally, only gasoline and distillate versions of the engine were offered, but later, diesel and LPG options were added. Either a hand or foot clutch could be ordered. The optional Western High-Altitude special consisted of a different front axle, rear fenders, oversized tires, and a hand clutch. The engine had a higher compression ratio, and the carburetor was supplied with smaller jets. A Riceland Special configuration was also available.

The Model 555 replaced the 55 in 1956. It was essentially the same as the 55, except for internal improvements such as the 12-volt electrical system (but not the two-range transmission power shift of other tractors in the Massey line).

SPECIFICATIONS

55 (diesel)

Engine: 4-cylinder, vertical, inline, overhead valve

Bore and stroke: 4.50×6.00 in.

Displacement: 382 ci., diesel fuel

Power: 54 drawbar hp, 60 belt hp; 5-plow rating

Transmission: 4f-1r

Top speed: 13.0 mph

Weight: 7,150 lb.

NTTL# 452

VARIATIONS

55 (1947–1956), 50 (1955–1956), 555 (1956–1958)

Massey-Harris 55 (diesel)

Minneapolis-Moline

Hopkins, Minnesota

In 1929, three companies—Minneapolis Steel and Machinery, the Minneapolis Threshing Machine Company, and the Moline Plow Company—merged to form the Minneapolis-Moline Power Implement Company. All three companies had made tractors in the years leading up to the merger, but only Minneapolis Steel and Machinery's Twin City line was carried forward. Originally, these tractors were labeled "Twin City" with "Minneapolis-Moline" added. Subsequently, the Minneapolis-Moline name supplanted the Twin City name. White Farm Equipment purchased Minneapolis-Moline in 1963 and dropped the M-M name in 1974.

Moline Universal D

MOLINE

UNIVERSAL MODEL D

Moline Plow's contribution to the tractor experience of the newly amalgamated Minneapolis-Moline Company was an all-purpose two-wheel machine that required a sulky, or a trailed implement, to hold up the back end. The driver sat on the sulky or implement, steering by articulation of the two elements. The Model D used a four-cylinder engine (some earlier versions used a two-cylinder horizontally opposed type). Pictures show some versions with water tanks in each wheel for added weight; others simply had cast cement in the wheels. The Universal used a unique electric governor-generator combination and a self-starter.

SPECIFICATIONS

Model D

Engine: 4-cylinder, vertical, inline, side valve

Bore and stroke: 3.50×5.00 in.

Displacement: 192 ci., gasoline fuel

Power: 17 drawbar hp, 28 belt hp; 2-plow rating

Transmission: 1f-1r

Top speed: 4 mph

Weight: 3,590 lb.

NTTL# 33

VARIATIONS

Universal D (1918–1923)

MINNEAPOLIS-MOLINE
MODELS KT, KTA, MT, AND MTA

The first original design from Minneapolis-Moline was the Universal KT ("Kombination Tractor") of 1930. It was a two-to-three-row cultivating tractor—by virtue of its arched wide front axle—with a four-cylinder engine, three-speed transmission, individual turning brakes, and a rear PTO.

Next, in 1931, came the MT Universal, a true tricycle row crop tractor with drop-box rear axles. This all-purpose tractor used a four-cylinder engine and three-speed gearbox. A host of mounted implements were available. In 1934, the MT was upgraded to the MTA, with the engine speed upped from 1,000 to 1,150 rpm. A high-compression gasoline head was an option, as were high-speed gears for rubber tires and a starter and lights.

Also in 1934, the improved KTA replaced the KT. Besides the universal, or row crop, version, an orchard version was available. These used the same engine as the Universal MT and MTA. "A" versions were not tested at the University of Nebraska.

1935 Minneapolis-Moline MTA

1930 Minneapolis-Moline KT

VARIATIONS

KT (1930–1934), KTA
(1934–1938), MT (1931–
1934), MTA (1934–1937)

MINNEAPOLIS-MOLINE
MODELS J, Z,
AND R

The Universal J, or JT, row crop tricycle came out in late 1934. Steering was by shaft and universal joint to a worm and sector gear in the front pedestal. Rather than drop boxes on the rear axles, larger wheels/tires and straight splined axles were used, adjustable in tread width. A four-cylinder F-head engine (intake valves were in head-exhaust valves in the block) was combined with a five-speed transmission, which gave the J a two-plow rating on either kerosene or gasoline. JTS standard-tread and JTO orchard versions were also available.

The Model Z was the first of the "Visionlined" styled M-Ms in new Prairie Gold and red livery. The cylinder head of the engine could be removed, and spacers could be added or removed to adjust the compression ratio for either gasoline or distillate fuel. Minneapolis-Moline was famous for their horizontal overhead-valve arrangement. With the camshaft in the block area, long rocker arms reached up to actuate the valves in the head. Pushrods, as such, were not required.

The Model R, available in row crop and standard-tread versions, had a four-speed transmission and used the same type of engine as the Z but with a shorter stroke. It was governed at a slower speed. A cab was an option.

SPECIFICATIONS
JT

Engine: 4-cylinder, vertical, inline, F-head

Bore and stroke: 3.63×4.75 in.

Displacement: 196 ci., kerosene fuel

Power: 17 drawbar hp, 23 belt hp; 2-plow rating

Transmission: 5f-1r

Top speed: 12 mph

Weight: 3,400 lb.

R

Engine: 4-cylinder, vertical, inline, overhead valve

Bore and stroke: 3.63×4.00 in.

Displacement: 165 ci., gasoline fuel

Power: 18 drawbar hp, 26 belt hp; 2-plow rating

Transmission: 5f-1r

Top speed: 13 mph

Weight: 3,414 lb.

NTTL# 468

VARIATIONS

JT (1934–1937), JTS/O (1936–1937), Z (1937–1956), R (1939–1954)

ABOVE Minneapolis-Moline JT, built between 1934 and 1937

TOP 1939 Minneapolis-Moline R

1941 Minneapolis-Moline GT

MODELS GT, GTA, GTB, GTC, GB, GBD, AND GVI

The Minneapolis-Moline GT, the big standard-tread plowing tractor, came out in 1939. The GT used a 403-cubic-inch four-cylinder engine with a four-speed transmission. In 1942, it was modernized as the GTA, and it was modernized again in 1947 and renamed the GTB, with the rated engine speed increased from 1,100 to 1,300 rpm.

The GTC debuted in 1951, equipped for burning LPG fuel. The final iteration, the GB, was introduced in 1954 (in both LPG and gasoline versions), as was the GBD, or GB Diesel. The GBD had a 426-cubic-inch six-cylinder Lanova-type diesel engine.

SPECIFICATIONS

GT

Engine: 4-cylinder, vertical, inline, overhead valve

Bore and stroke: 4.63×6.00 in.

Displacement: 403 ci., gasoline fuel

Power: 37 drawbar hp, 54 belt hp; 4-plow rating

Transmission: 4f-1r

Top speed: 10 mph

Weight: 6,837 lb.

1955 Minneapolis-Moline GBD

GBD production ended in 1959 when replaced by the Gvi—still with 426-cubic-inch diesel, with power upped to 79 horsepower. About the only difference was that the engine speed changed from 1,300 to 1,500 rpm.

All versions except the original GT were equipped with five-speed transmissions. These tractors had bare weights of around 8,000 pounds; working weights were closer to 12,000 pounds.

GBD

Engine: 6-cylinder, vertical, inline, overhead valve

Bore and stroke: 4.25×5.00 in.

Displacement: 426 ci., diesel fuel

Power: 44 drawbar hp, 63 belt hp; 5-plow rating

Transmission: 5f-1r

Top speed: 15 mph

Weight: 8,170 lb.

NTTL# 568

VARIATIONS

GT (1939–1942), GTA (1942–1947), GTB (1947–1954), GTC (1951–1953), GB (1954–1959), GBD (1954–1959), Gvi (1959–1962)

MINNEAPOLIS-MOLINE
MODELS BF, V,
AND BG

The Minneapolis-Moline Model BF started life as the Cletrac General GG. It was a small, lightweight unit with a 123-cubic-inch Hercules four-cylinder engine, and it was built for Cletrac by B. F. Avery & Sons Co. of Louisville, Kentucky. The General GG was produced in small quantities until 1945, when B. F. Avery bought the rights from Cletrac and renamed it the Avery Model A. At the same time, the engine was changed to a 133-cubic-inch Hercules. The Avery A, like the General GG, had only a single front wheel. In the 1940s, Montgomery Ward and Massey-Harris also sold versions of it.

Avery added a smaller wide-front version in 1946, called the Model V, a one-plow outfit that used a four-cylinder 65-cubic-inch Hercules engine, but with the same

SPECIFICATIONS

BF

Engine: 4-cylinder, vertical, inline, side valve

Bore and stroke: 3.63×4.00 in.

Displacement: 133 ci., gasoline fuel

Power: 19 drawbar hp, 27 belt hp; 2-plow rating

Transmission: 4f-1r

Top speed: 13 mph

Weight: 2,894 lb.

NTTL# 469

1951 Minneapolis-Moline BF

1952 Minneapolis-Moline V

basic configuration as the A. In 1950, Avery changed the designation of the Model A to the Model R, which was now offered with a four-speed transmission, hydraulics, adjustable rear-wheel treads, and three interchangeable front-end types.

In 1951, Minneapolis-Moline took over B. F. Avery. Since M-M already had a Model R, the Avery tractor was relabeled as the Model BF.

The little V continued unchanged by M-M until 1953, when the Model BG replaced it. The BG was close to being the same as the BF, except that it was narrower and still intended to be a single-row tractor. Starter and lights were optional.

V

Engine: 4-cylinder, vertical, inline, side valve

Bore and stroke: 3.62×3.00 in.

Displacement: 65 ci., gasoline fuel

Power: 9 drawbar hp, 12 belt hp; 1-plow rating

Transmission: 3f-1r

Top speed: 7 mph

Weight: 1,800 lb.

VARIATIONS

BF (1951–1955), V (1951–1953), BG (1953–1955)

1955 Minneapolis-Moline 445 Utility

MINNEAPOLIS-MOLINE
MODELS 445
AND JET STAR

The Minneapolis-Moline Model 445 was both a row crop and a utility-configuration tractor, introduced in 1956. It was restyled as the Jet Star in 1960. The Jet Star was only available in the utility configuration; otherwise it was the same as the 445 under the skin. All versions were equipped with a class 2 three-point hitch with draft control, live hydraulics and PTO, a five-speed transmission, and in gasoline, LPG, or diesel-fueled engines of 206 cubic inches—the same basic engine used in the M-M Model Z. The Jet Star was available with an optional partial-range power shift called the Ampli-Torc and in either two- or four-wheel drive. It was not tested at the University of Nebraska (the Model 445 was, however). The Jet Star 2 replaced the Jet Star in 1962, with only styling changes.

SPECIFICATIONS

445

Engine: 4-cylinder, vertical, inline, overhead valve

Bore and stroke: 3.63×5.00 in.

Displacement: 206 ci., gasoline fuel

Power: 31 drawbar hp, 40 belt hp; 3-plow rating

Transmission: 10f-2r

Top speed: 15 mph

Weight: 4,600 lb.

NTTL# 579

1960 Minneapolis-Moline Jet Star

VARIATIONS

445 (1956–1959), Jet Star
(1960–1961), Jet Star 2
(1962–1963)

Hart-Parr & Oliver

Charles City, Iowa

When Charles Parr enrolled as an engineering student at the University of Wisconsin in Madison, he was pursuing his dream of harnessing mechanical power to farming. At UW, he met Charles Hart, also an engineering student—and he infected Hart with his enthusiasm for the internal combustion engine. Together, and with the help of their instructors, they built several working engines. Before graduating with honors in 1897, they formed the Hart-Parr Gasoline Engine Company, with a factory in Madison. In 1900, they moved their operation to Charles City, Iowa, Hart's hometown, where money for expansion could be obtained.

By 1902, their first "traction engine" (the term used before "tractor"), Hart-Parr Number 1, was operating and producing 30 belt horsepower, or pulling up to five 14-inch plow bottoms. Hart-Parr is credited with developing oil-cooled engines, the overhead-valve engine principle, magneto ignition, and the use of kerosene fuel. They are also credited with coining the word "tractor" in their advertising.

By 1905, Hart and Parr had established the only business in America devoted exclusively to tractor production. Within two years, one-third of all American tractors were Hart-Parrs.

Thirty-seven years earlier, James Oliver, a plow maker in Mishawaka, Indiana, had patented his Oliver Chilled Plow after many years of development. Ordinary cast-iron plows had surface imperfections that led to soil adhesion and high draft loads. Steel plows were effective but much more expensive. Oliver's chilling scheme, once developed, left a hard surface on the mold board that could be polished to a high shine and a surface smoothness that exceeded that of steel.

The Oliver Chilled Plow Company merged with Hart-Parr in 1929, becoming the Oliver Farm Equipment Company. The plow and implement factory remained in Mishawaka, while the tractor factory stayed in Charles City. The company changed its name in 1944 to the Oliver Corporation. In 1960, the White Motor Corporation took over Oliver, and the Oliver name disappeared.

HART-PARR
NO. 1 AND 30-60

The 1902 Hart-Parr No. 1 was the first of a series that used one- and two-cylinder oil-cooled engines. Some fifteen variations of the original were sold, the last being the Model 18-35. Production switched to the now-conventional water cooling in 1918.

The "Old Reliable" Model 30-60 appeared in 1907. It weighed a little more than 20,000 pounds and was one of the most successful of the series, continuing in production through 1918. Other sizes were also built during this period. But it was the 30-60 that put the company on the map.

Oil was used as a cooling medium, since it has a higher boiling temperature than water. Higher temperatures were required for successfully burning kerosene fuels. The cooling tower radiator was a hallmark of the Hart-Parr oil-cooled tractors.

SPECIFICATIONS

30-60

Engine: 2-cylinder, horizontal, side by side, overhead valve

Bore and stroke: 10×15 in.

Displacement: 2,356 ci., kerosene fuel

Power: 30 drawbar hp, 60 belt hp; 8-plow rating

Transmission: 1f-1r

Top speed: 2.3 mph

Weight: 20,500 lb.

VARIATIONS

No. 1 (1902), 17-30 (1903–1906), 22-45 (1903–1906), 30-60 (1907–1918), 40-80 (1909–1912), 20-40 (1912–1914), 18-35 (1915–1918)

1915 Hart-Parr 30-60

OLIVER HART-PARR
MODELS 18-27
AND 18-28

In 1930, right after the merger, Oliver Hart-Parr brought out all-new standard-tread and row crop tractors. Featured were vertical four-cylinder engines and three-speed transmissions. Prior to testing at the University of Nebraska, these tractors were simply identified as the Oliver Hart-Parr 2-3, since they were capable of handling two 14-inch plows in most soil and three in some soils. Once the tractors were tested and assigned drawbar and belt horsepower ratings, those rating numbers were adopted as the official identities—18-28 for the standard-tread and 18-27 for the row crop—since tractors were commonly identified by their rating numbers at the time. Although performance was essentially the same for both, the numbers for the row crop were slightly altered in order to avoid confusion between the two styles.

The engines and transmissions were the same for both the 18-27 and 18-28. The 18-27 was originally built with a single front wheel, with a dual-tricycle option added later. Rear wheels for the 18-27 had a new Oliver design called "skeleton" or "Tip-Toe" wheels (wheels made with little or no face, just lugs on a flat plate—good for traction in dry soils).

SPECIFICATIONS

18-28

Engine: 4-cylinder, vertical, inline, overhead valve

Bore and stroke: 4.13×5.25 in.

Displacement: 280 ci., kerosene fuel

Power: 24 drawbar hp, 30 belt hp; 2-plow rating

Transmission: 3f-1r

Top speed: 4 mph

Weight: 4,420 lb.

NTTL# 180

VARIATIONS

18-28 and 18-27 (both 1930–1937)

Oliver Hart-Parr 18-28, built in the 1930s

1937 Oliver 70

OLIVER
MODELS 70, 77, SUPER 77, AND 770

The introduction of the Oliver Model 70 in 1935 marked one of the most profound turning points in farm implement industry. Besides the strikingly handsome styling, the 70 had a self-starter, generator, battery, lights, convenient controls, and—most unheard of—a six-cylinder engine! The HC (high compression) engine was designed to run on 70-octane gasoline, commonly available at the time. A KD (kerosene) version offered less horsepower. The 1935–1936 versions had four-speed transmissions for row crop tractors and six-speed units for standard-tread and orchard versions.

For 1937, the Model 70 was restyled under Oliver's Fleetline styling concept—"Fleetline" was Oliver's trademark name for new streamlined sheet metal covering the tractor's mechanism—but the tractor was essentially the same under the skin. The Airport 25, a variation offered for

SPECIFICATIONS
70 HC

Engine: 6-cylinder, vertical, inline, overhead valve

Bore and stroke: 3.13×4.38 in.

Displacement: 202 ci., gasoline fuel

Power: 18 drawbar hp, 26 belt hp; 2-plow rating

Transmission: 4f-1r

Top speed: 6 mph

Weight: 3,500 lb.

NTTL# 252

airport operations, was a standard-tread incorporating an electrical system (an option on ag models), a side exhaust, front and rear drawbars, and both foot and hand brakes. In 1939, six-speed transmission (two in reverse) was made standard for all of the 70s, along with the locations and sizes for hitches and PTOs that had been newly specified by the American Society of Agricultural Engineers (ASAE).

In 1947, New Fleetline styling (revised grille and side panels) and a double numbering system were introduced, and the Model 70 became the Model 77. It was initially available in high- or low-compression alternates, but in 1949, a diesel version replaced the kerosene burner, and in 1952, an LPG version was added. Also in 1949, the Hydra-Lectric lift system, meant to counter inroads made by the Ford-Ferguson three-point hitch, was an added option, providing either electric or manual control of implements.

The Oliver Super 77 replaced the 77 in 1954. It offered a three-point hitch and an adjustable wide-front row crop option. It was available with gasoline-, LPG-, or diesel-fueled engines and in row crop, orchard, high crop, industrial, and standard-tread types.

Three-number identifiers came out in 1958, and the Model 77 became the 770. It had a new color scheme, with new green and an almost-white paint for the wheels. Engine speed and compression ratios were increased to give more power across the board, and the new half-step power shift auxiliary transmission doubled the ratios available.

770

Engine: 6-cylinder, vertical, inline, overhead valve

Bore and stroke: 3.50×3.75 in.

Displacement: 216 ci., gasoline fuel

Power: 35 drawbar hp, 48 belt hp; 4-plow rating

Transmission: 6f-2r

Top speed: 11 mph

Weight: 5,945 lb.

NTTL# 648

VARIATIONS

70 (1940–1948), 77 (1948–1954), Super 77 (1954–1958), 770 (1959–1964)

1961 Oliver 770

1938 Oliver 80 Row Crop

OLIVER
MODELS 80, 88, SUPER 88, AND 880

The Oliver 80 row crop and standard were introduced in late 1937 as an outgrowth of the Oliver Hart-Parr 18-27 and 18-28. The four-cylinder engine was the same, except that the bore was larger, and for the kerosene version it was a quarter inch greater than that of the gasoline version, equalizing the power output at about 38 horsepower. In 1940, a four-speed transmission was added, and in 1942 a diesel became available.

SPECIFICATIONS
80 HC

Engine: 4-cylinder, vertical, inline, overhead valve

Bore and stroke: 4.25×5.25 in.

Displacement: 298 ci., gasoline fuel

Power: 33 drawbar, 38 belt hp; 3-plow rating

Transmission: 4f-1r

Top speed: 6 mph

Weight: 5,130 lb.

NTTL# 365

The Model 88 came out in 1947 in Fleetline styling, with a six-cylinder engine and six-speed transmission. Oliver six-speed transmission provided two reverse speeds as well. The 88 was changed to New Fleetline styling in mid-1948, coinciding with Oliver's one-hundredth anniversary.

The first Oliver tractor to top 50 horsepower on the belt was the Super 88. The 265-cubic-inch version of the six-cylinder engine was used for gasoline and diesel fuels, and the distillate engine was dropped. Engine side panels were not used on the Super series, which had light green, rather than red, wheels.

Improvements for the Model 880 were a more powerful engine coupled with the Power-Booster half-ratio power shift and Power-Traction three-point hitch.

These Oliver tractors were sold in Canada under the Cockshutt banner (see page 162).

880

Engine: 6-cylinder, vertical, inline, overhead valve

Bore and stroke: 3.75×4.00 in.

Displacement: 265 ci., gasoline fuel

Power: 42 drawbar hp, 57 belt hp; 4-plow rating

Transmission: 6f-2r

Top speed: 11 mph

Weight: 5,631 lb.

NTTL# 647

VARIATIONS

80 Unstyled (1938–1947), 88 Fleetline (1947–1948), 88 New Fleetline (1948–1954), Super 88 (1954–1958), 880 (1958–1963)

Oliver 880, built between 1958 and 1963

OLIVER
MODELS 60, 66, SUPER 66, AND 660

In 1940, Oliver brought out the Model 60, a smaller version of the popular Model 70, but with a four-cylinder engine and four-speed transmission. It was styled in Fleetline trim. Only a row crop was initially offered, but in 1942, a standard-tread version was added. Gasoline and distillate engine configurations were available. Rubber tires were standard, with steel wheels as an option.

The Model 60 became the Model 66 in 1947. It was initially available in high- or low-compression engines of 129 cubic inches, replacing the 120-cubic-inch unit. In 1952, an LPG version was added. The Hydra-Lectric system (see page 146) became an option in 1949.

SPECIFICATIONS

60 HC

Engine: 4-cylinder, vertical, inline, overhead valve

Bore and stroke: 3.31×3.50 in.

Displacement: 120 ci., gasoline fuel

Power: 15 drawbar hp, 18 belt hp; 2-plow rating

Transmission: 4f-1r

Top speed: 6 mph

Weight: 2,450 lb.

NTTL# 375

1945 Oliver 60 Row Crop

1948 Oliver Super 66

The Oliver Super 66 replaced the 66 in 1954. It offered the Hydra-Lectric lift three-point hitch, providing either electric or manual implement control, and it had an adjustable wide-front row crop option. Also new were the six-speed transmission and three governor speeds: 1,600 rpm for PTO work, 1,750 for drawbar work, and 2,000 for belt pulley work. Green, instead of red, wheels were used on row crop tractors.

The restyled 660 replaced the Super 66 in 1959. Row crop types offered single-wheel, dual-tricycle, or adjustable wide fronts. Rear wheels were power-adjustable for tread width. Double disk brakes were standard equipment, and power steering was optional.

Super 66 Diesel

Engine: 4-cylinder, vertical, inline, overhead valve

Bore and stroke: 3.50×3.75 in.

Displacement: 144 ci., diesel fuel

Power: 23 drawbar hp, 34 belt hp; 2-plow rating

Transmission: 6f-2r

Top speed: 11 mph

Weight: 4,050 lb.

NTTL# 544

VARIATIONS

60 (1940–1948), 66 (1948–1954), Super 66 (1954–1958), 660 (1959–1964)

MODELS 28-44, 90, 99, SUPER 99, SUPER 99GM, 950, 990, AND 995

The Oliver Hart-Parr 28-44 was a big, robust plowing tractor capable of handling five 14-inch plows. The name changed to Oliver 90 in 1937. Still later, it became the Model 99, but with high-pressure lubrication, a self-starter, a central rear PTO, and a governor. A new four-speed transmission was used, and a gasoline-fueled version was added. In 1952, the engine was changed to a six, with 302-cubic-inch displacement in both gasoline and diesel versions. It had the longest production run of any Oliver tractor, ending in 1957.

The Super 99 was available with the six-cylinder gasoline engine or six-cylinder Oliver diesel, both of which displaced 302 cubic inches. The Super 99GM used a three-cylinder General Motors two-cycle diesel in place of the Oliver unit. Both tractors used a six-speed transmission, with a torque converter as an option.

SPECIFICATIONS
28-44

Engine: 4-cylinder, vertical, inline, overhead valve

Bore and stroke: 4.75×6.25 in.

Displacement: 443 ci., kerosene fuel

Power: 28 drawbar hp, 49 belt hp; 5-plow rating

Transmission: 3f-1r

Top speed: 4 mph

Weight: 6,415 lb.

NTTL# 183

995 GM Lugmatic

Engine: 3-cylinder, 2-cycle, vertical, inline, overhead exhaust valve

Bore and stroke: 4.25×5.00 in.

Displacement: 213 ci., diesel fuel

Power: 61 drawbar hp, 85 belt hp; 8-plow rating

Transmission: 6f-2r

Top speed: 14 mph

Weight: 11,245 lb.

NTTL# 662

8-12 1958 Oliver Super 99 GM Diesel

The Model 950 was a restyled Super 99, using the same gasoline or diesel six-cylinder engine. The 990 replaced the Super 99GM. It was the same except that governed speed rose from 1,600 to 1,800 rpm, and it was restyled to reflect the current corporate theme. Except for the addition of a Lugmatic torque converter and an increase in governed speed to 2,000 rpm, the 995 was the same as the 990.

VARIATIONS

28-44 (1930–1937), 90 (1937–1952), 99 (1952–1957), Super 99, Super 99GM (both 1957–1958), 950, 990, 995 (all 1958–1961)

OLIVER
MODELS SUPER 55 AND 550

Oliver brought out the Super 55 in 1954. It was one of numerous utility-configuration tractors released by manufacturers following the popularity of Ford and Ferguson tractors, all of which featured the three-point hitch with draft control. The Super 55 offered either gasoline or diesel power from a 144-cubic-inch four-cylinder engine, the gasoline version using a compression ratio of 7:1—a new high for gasoline tractors, and a factor in improving fuel economy. The Oliver six-speed transmission was used for all versions.

In 1958, production shifted to the new Model 550. Unlike the Super 55, the 550 could be ordered with fixed wheel treads. In addition to restyling and minor improvements, the 550 had an increased engine displacement, from 144 to 155 cubic inches, by increasing the bore diameter. A two-speed PTO was an added feature, as was optional power steering.

Oliver Super 55 Diesel, built between 1954 and 1958

SPECIFICATIONS

Super 55 Diesel

Engine: 4-cylinder, vertical, inline, overhead valve

Bore and stroke: 3.50×3.75 in.

Displacement: 144 ci., diesel fuel

Power: 23 drawbar, 34 belt hp; 2-plow rating

Transmission: 6f-2r

Top speed: 13 mph

Weight: 3,476 lb.

NTTL# 526

1959 Model 550

Engine: 4-cylinder, vertical, inline, overhead valve

Bore and stroke: 3.63×3.25 in.

Displacement: 155 ci., gasoline fuel

Power: 28 drawbar hp, 41 belt hp; 2-plow rating

Transmission: 6f-2r

Top speed: 15 mph

Weight: 3,655 lb.

NTTL# 697

VARIATIONS

Super 55 (1954–1958), 550 (1958–1975)

OLIVER
MODELS SUPER 44 AND 440

The Oliver Super 44, introduced in 1957, was built with a configuration like that of the Farmall Model A, with the driver seat and steering wheel offset to the right. The engine was a departure for Oliver: it was a side-valve 140-cubic-inch unit by Continental, rather than the traditional Oliver overhead-valve type. A four-speed transmission was provided, as was a built-in hydraulic system to operate the three-point hitch and remote cylinders.

The 440 Model was merely a designation change for the year 1960, to make the designator similar to that of others in the line. Otherwise, the 440 was essentially the same as the Super 44. Neither the Super 44 nor the 440 were submitted to the University of Nebraska for testing.

SPECIFICATIONS

Super 44 and Oliver 440

Engine: 4-cylinder, vertical, inline, side valve

Bore and stroke: 3.20×4.40 in.

Displacement: 140 ci., gasoline fuel

Power: 10 drawbar hp, 16 belt hp; 1-plow rating

Transmission: 4f-1r

Top speed: 7 mph

Weight: 2,000 lb.

1957 Oliver Super 44

1960 Oliver 440

VARIATIONS

Super 44 (1957–1959),
440 (1960–1975)

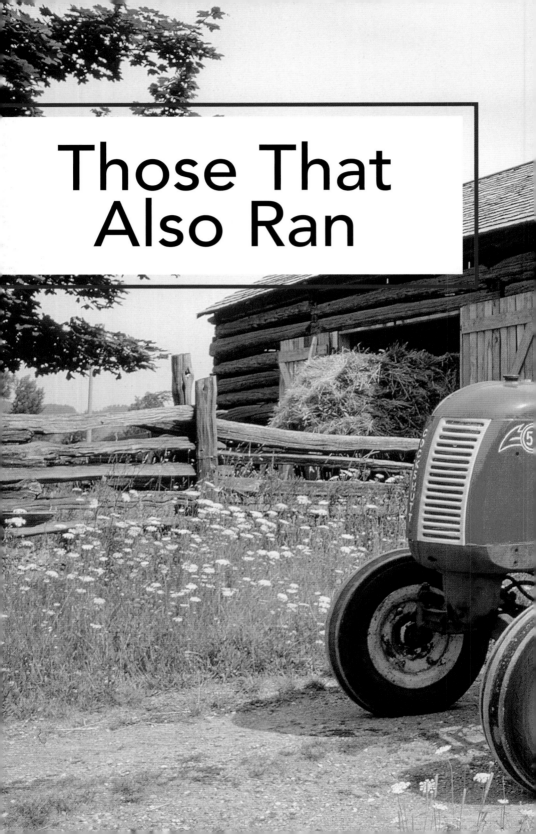

Those That Also Ran

Advance-Rumely

La Porte, Indiana

The Advance-Rumely Thresher Company was located in La Porte, Indiana, but kept a factory in Mansfield, Ohio. The Rumely portion of Advance-Rumely had its beginnings before the American Civil War making threshers and steam engines. The first internal combustion "OilPull" tractor was built by Rumely in 1910. Oil was used as the cooling medium because of its higher boiling temperature than water. OilPull became the tractor's trade name.

Rumely bought the Advance Thresher Company, based in Battle Creek, Michigan, in 1911, and the Aultman-Taylor Machinery Company, in Mansfield, Ohio, in 1924. OilPull tractors remained in the line until 1928, when they were replaced by DoAll convertible cultivator/tractors. In June 1931, at the depths of the Great Depression, Allis-Chalmers bought the failing Advance-Rumely.

ADVANCE-RUMELY
OILPULL TYPES
E 30-60 AND
G 20-40

Advance-Rumely's OilPull Model Type E 30-60 featured a two-cylinder horizontal side-by-side transverse engine operating at 375 rpm. A single speed in forward and reverse was provided in the transmission. Engine cylinders were offset from the crankshaft centerline to reduce piston side loads. Water injection kept combustion-chamber temperatures reasonable; sometimes as much water as fuel was consumed. High-tension magneto ignitions were used except on the earliest versions. A centrifugal pump circulated cooling oil. Engine exhaust was used to induce airflow through a chimney-type radiator.

The OilPull line was noted for its large-displacement slow turning engines. OilPull tractors could generally best their official power and pull ratings, endearing them to their owners.

SPECIFICATIONS
Type E 30-60

Engine: 2-cylinder, horizontal, transverse, overhead valve

Bore and stroke: 10.00×12.00 in.

Displacement: 1,885 ci., kerosene fuel

Power: 50 drawbar hp, 76 belt hp; 8-plow rating

Transmission: 1f-1r

Top speed: 2 mph

Weight: 26,000 lb.

NTTL# 8

1913 Rumely OilPull 30-60

1923 Advance-Rumely OilPull G 20-40

One of the most successful OilPulls was the Type G 20-40, conservatively rated at 20 horsepower on the drawbar and 40 on the belt. It was built like the bigger Type E, but it used a two-speed transmission. It was in Rumely's inventory from 1920 to 1924.

Type G 20-40

Engine: 2-cylinder, horizontal, transverse, overhead valve

Bore and stroke: 8.00×10.00 in.

Displacement: 1,005 ci., kerosene fuel

Power: 30 drawbar hp, 46 belt hp; 4-plow rating

Transmission: 2f-1r

Top speed: 3 mph

Weight: 12,969 lb.

NTTL# 11

VARIATIONS

Type E (1911–1923), Type G (1920–1924)

ADVANCE-RUMELY
DOALL AND
MODEL 6A

The Rumely DoAll line came after Advance-Rumely acquired convertible tractor patents from the Minneapolis-based Toro Manufacturing Company, a maker of golf course– and turf-maintenance equipment, in 1927. The design was originally available in two styles: one was convertible from a tractor to a motor cultivator, the other nonconvertible. In either case, it was a nominal 20-horsepower machine using a Waukesha four-cylinder engine and two-speed transmission. Toro went on to become famous for mowers and golf-course equipment.

The Rumely Model 6A came out in 1930 with a six-cylinder Waukesha-designed engine and three-speed transmission. The 6A was introduced shortly before the Allis-Chalmers take-over, and it remained in Allis-Chalmers catalogs until 1934.

SPECIFICATIONS
DoAll

Engine: 4-cylinder, vertical, inline, side valve

Bore and stroke: 3.50×4.50 in.

Displacement: 173 ci., gasoline fuel

Power: 15 drawbar hp, 20 belt hp; 2-plow rating

Transmission: 2f-1r

Top speed: 4 mph

Weight: 3,000 lb.

6A

Engine: 6-cylinder, vertical, inline, side valve

Bore and stroke: 4.25×4.75 in.

Displacement: 202 ci., gasoline fuel

Power: 34 drawbar hp, 48 belt hp; 4-plow rating

Transmission: 3f-1r

Top speed: 5 mph

Weight: 6,000 lb.

NTTL# 185

VARIATIONS

DoAll (1928–1931), 6A (1930–1934)

1931 Advance-Rumely 6A

Cockshutt

Brantford, Ontario

James G. Cockshutt started the Cockshutt Plow Company of Brantford, Ontario, in 1877. The company became famous for a novel sulky plow, patented in the late 1870s. Besides plows, also on offer were disks, planters, cultivators, and other types of farm equipment. James Cockshutt's descendants managed the company until 1957 (renamed the Cockshutt Farm Equipment Company Ltd. in 1950), when the English Transcontinental Company took over. Transcontinental liquidated assets, and by 1961, remaining equipment was sold to the White Motor Corporation. White, which had acquired Oliver and Minneapolis-Moline, assigned Canadian dealerships to Cockshutt and US dealerships to Oliver/Minneapolis Moline. The Cockshutt plant in Brantford manufactured combines for various sales organizations, while tractors were manufactured in Charles City, Iowa. Tractors for Canada though Olivers, were painted in Cockshutt colors and used the Cockshutt name.

1942 Cockshutt 30

COCKSHUTT
MODEL 30

The Model 30 was the first proprietary tractor by Cockshutt, in production from 1946 to 1957. (Previously, Cockshutt had imported Oliver tractors painted in Cockshutt livery.) It was the first Canadian-built tractor tested at the University of Nebraska. It was also one of the first—if not the first—tractors to incorporate a live power take-off (PTO). Hydraulic power for implement lift was an option. Illinois's Buda Engine Company supplied the four-cylinder engine. A four-speed transmission was incorporated, but an underdrive auxiliary was optional, giving eight speeds forward and two in reverse. Initially only gasoline and distillate fuel versions were supplied, but in the 1950s, Buda diesel and LPG engines were added. Customers had a choice of row crop single, narrow, or wide front ends. The Model 30 was sold in the United States as the CO-OP E3 and Gamble Farmcrest 30 from 1947 to 1950. Only the Cockshutt Model 30 (gasoline) was tested at the University of Nebraska.

SPECIFICATIONS

30

Engine: 4-cylinder, vertical, inline, overhead valve

Bore and stroke: 3.44×4.13 in.

Displacement: 153 ci., gasoline fuel

Power: 22 drawbar hp, 30 PTO hp; 3-plow rating

Transmission: 4f-1r, or 8f-2r

Top speed: 10–12 mph

Weight: 3,609 lb.

NTTL# 382

1948 Cockshutt CO-OP E3

VARIATIONS

30 (1946–1957), CO-OP
E3 (1947–1950), Gamble
Farmcrest 30 (1947–1950),
30 LPG and Diesel (1951–
1957)

COCKSHUTT
MODELS 40, 50, AND 35

The Cockshutt 40, besides being somewhat larger than the 30, was distinguished by its over-the-engine steering arrangement. It used a Buda 230-cubic-inch six-cylinder engine in gasoline, distillate, and diesel fuel versions. The transmission had six speeds forward and two in reverse. Narrow and wide front ends were available, and live PTO and hydraulics were options. The 40 was sold in the United States as the CO-OP E4.

SPECIFICATIONS

40

Engine: 6-cylinder, vertical, inline, overhead valve

Bore and stroke: 3.44×4.13 in.

Displacement: 230 ci., gasoline fuel

Power: 30 drawbar hp, 41 belt hp; 3-plow rating

Transmission: 6f-1r

Top speed: 12.0 mph

Weight: 5,305 lb.

NTTL# 442

1958 Cockshutt 40 Deluxe Gasoline

1954 Cockshutt 50 Diesel

The Cockshutt 50 and 50D (diesel) were added to the line in 1953. They were the same as the 40, except that the engine displacement was increased to 273 cubic inches by omitting the cylinder sleeves. No distillate version of the 50 was offered. The 50 became the CO-OP E5 in the United States.

In 1953, Cockshutt switched engines: the 40 was changed to a four-cylinder Perkins diesel of 269.5 cubic inches. Its name changed to 40D4 in Canada and Golden Eagle in the United States. At the same time, a Hercules 198-cubic-inch engine was installed in the 40, which was redesignated 35 (Canada) and Blackhawk 35 (United States). This tractor then replaced the 30 series.

50 (Diesel)

Engine: 6-cylinder, vertical, inline, overhead valve

Bore and stroke: 3.75×4.13 in.

Displacement: 273 ci., diesel fuel

Power: 36 drawbar hp, 56 belt hp; 4-plow rating

Transmission: 6f-1r

Top speed: 10.0 mph

Weight: 6,163 lb.

NTTL# 487

VARIATIONS

40 (1949–1957), 50 (1953–1957)

COCKSHUTT
MODEL 20

The Cockshutt 20, also designated the CO-OP E2, began life in 1952 with a Continental side-valve engine of 124-cubic-inch displacement. This proved to be somewhat inadequate, so before a full year of production, the bore was increased from 3.00 inches to 3.19 inches. The stroke remained 4.38 inches; therefore the displacement was increased to 140 cubic inches. Both distillate and gasoline versions of the engine were available. The 20 was equipped with a four-speed transmission. Hydraulics and a live PTO were options. The diminutive 20 had a basic weight of only about 2,800 pounds, yet in its Nebraska test, it was able to pull 3,300 pounds in its maximum drawbar pull test. Of course, some 1,600 pounds of ballast were added for the test. This model was produced until the Model 540 replaced it in 1958.

1952 Cockshutt 20

SPECIFICATIONS
20 (Early)

Engine: 4-cylinder, vertical, inline, side valve

Bore and stroke: 3.00×4.38 in.

Displacement: 124 ci., gasoline fuel

Power: 17 drawbar hp, 24 belt hp; 2-plow rating

Transmission: 4f-1r

Top speed: 12 mph

Weight: 2,785 lb.

20 (Late)

Engine: 4-cylinder, vertical, inline, side valve

Bore and stroke: 3.19×4.38 in.

Displacement: 140 ci., gasoline fuel

Power: 20 drawbar hp, 27 belt hp; 2-plow rating

Transmission: 4f-1r

Top speed: 13.0 mph

Weight: 2,813 lb.

NTTL# 474

COCKSHUTT
540, 550, 560, AND 570

For the 1958 model year, the Cockshutt lineup of tractors received a complete modernization. Famous industrial designer Raymond Loewy created the crisp new styling. The 540 (gasoline only) replaced the 20; the 550 (gas or diesel) replaced the 35; the 560 (diesel only) replaced the 40D4; and the 570 (gas or diesel) replaced the 50. All used six-speed transmissions without auxiliaries.

SPECIFICATIONS

550 Diesel

Engine: 4-cylinder, vertical, inline, overhead valve

Bore and stroke: 3.75×4.50 in.

Displacement: 198 ci., diesel fuel

Power: 35 drawbar hp, 39 PTO hp; 3-plow rating

Transmission: 6f-1r

Top speed: 14 mph

Weight: 5,695 lb.

NTTL# 681

570 Diesel

Engine: 6-cylinder, vertical, inline, overhead valve

Bore and stroke: 3.75×4.50 in.

Displacement: 298 ci., diesel fuel

Power: 41 drawbar hp, 61 PTO hp; 5-plow rating

Transmission: 6f-1r

Top speed: 13 mph

Weight: 7,175 lb.

NTTL# 683

VARIATIONS

540, 550, 560, 570 (all 1958–1962)

1961 Cockshutt 570 Super

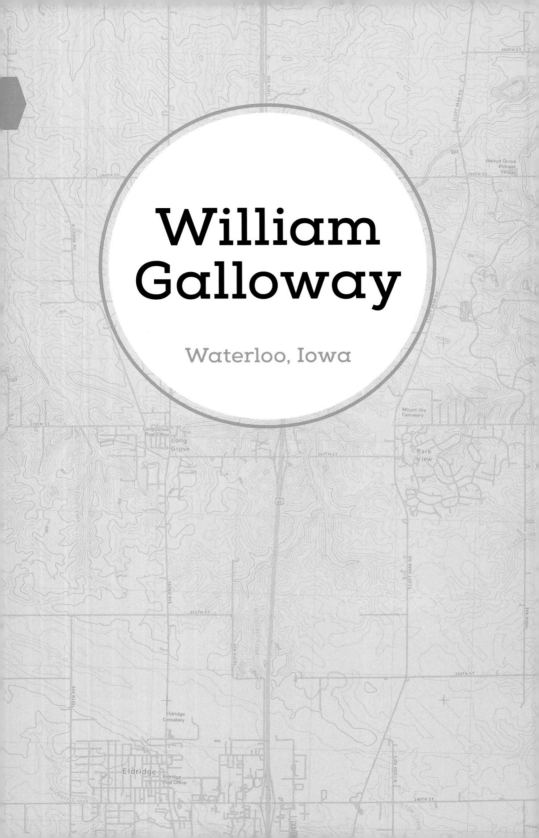

William Galloway

Waterloo, Iowa

1914 Galloway Farmobile

GALLOWAY
FARMOBILE

The William Galloway Company was in the engine and automobile business in the early 1900s. Originally, a Maytag-brand automobile was manufactured, but when it did not sell well, Galloway and Maytag split, and Maytag began manufacturing washing machines. By 1916, Galloway began marketing his Galloway Farmobile tractor, which somewhat resembled the Waterloo Boy (see page 43). Sales were fairly vigorous until World War I but did not survive postwar competition. The tractor was conventional for the time, using a four-cylinder engine mounted crosswise of Galloway's own design, as well as a two-speed transmission. Automobile-type steering was used.

The William Galloway Company went bankrupt in 1920.

SPECIFICATIONS

Farmobile

Engine: 4-cylinder, horizontal, transverse, overhead valve

Bore and stroke: 4.50×5.00 in.

Displacement: 318 ci., kerosene fuel

Power: 12 drawbar hp, 20 belt hp; 2-plow rating

Transmission: 2f-1r

Top speed: 2.3 mph

Weight: 5,450 lb.

Graham-Paige

Detroit, Michigan

GRAHAM
BRADLEY MODEL 503-103

Two versions of this streamlined tractor debuted in 1938: a tricycle row crop, Model 503-103, and a standard tread, Model 503-104. Production seems to have been limited to 1938 and 1939; possibly some were made in 1940, but the 1941 *Tractor Field Book* lists them as being out of production. The six-cylinder engine was the same as that used in the Graham-Paige automobile, although in this case, it was limited to 1,500 rpm. The company rated the tractor for two 14-inch plow bottoms. It was equipped with starter and lights, a hydraulic lift, and a unique four-speed belt pulley. The Sears, Roebuck catalog marketed the 503, they imposed the "Bradley" name, their brand of farm products.

After World War II, Graham-Paige was folded into the new Kaiser-Frazer Corporation, and tractor production was shelved in favor of marketing a new line of automobiles.

SPECIFICATIONS
503-103

Engine: 6-cylinder, vertical, inline, side valve

Bore and stroke: 3.25×4.38 in.

Displacement: 214 ci., gasoline fuel

Power: 21 drawbar hp, 30 belt hp; 2-plow rating

Transmission: 4f-1r

Top speed: 20 mph

Weight: 5,000 lb.

1938 Graham-Bradley 503-103

Intercontinental

Grand Prairie,
Texas

1948 Intercontinental C-26

INTERCONTINENTAL
MODEL C-26

The Intercontinental Manufacturing Company of Grand Prairie, Texas (near Dallas), introduced their first tractor offering in 1948. It was a conventional row crop tricycle machine identified as the Model C-26. A Continental Red Seal four-cylinder engine of 162-cubic-inch displacement powered the C-26. The rear wheels were adjustable in tread width. Standard equipment included fenders, a starter, PTO, and belt pulley. A hydraulic lift system was optional. Several diesel versions were also offered.

Following the lifting of World War II manufacturing restrictions, traditional tractor makers returned to the market, and the company went out of the tractor business around 1950.

SPECIFICATIONS
C-26

Engine: 4-cylinder, vertical, inline, side valve

Bore and stroke: 3.44×4.38 in.

Displacement: 162 ci., gasoline fuel

Power: 20 drawbar hp, 28 belt hp; 2-plow rating

Transmission: 4f-1r

Top speed: 11 mph

Weight: 3,100 lb.

NTTL# 400

Leader

Chagrin Falls, Ohio

LEADER
MODELS A THROUGH D

The Leader Tractor Manufacturing Company's home was actually in Auburn, Ohio, but since Auburn had no post office, they claimed Chagrin Falls. Lewis Brockway started the company in 1940. The first Leaders were small garden tractors of his own design, powered by rebuilt four-cylinder Chevrolet engines from the 1920s. The first Model A also used the Chevy engine, but when supply of the old engines ran out, Brockway switched to the six-cylinder Chrysler engine, available during wartime but somewhat overkill for the small tractor. After the war, the Leader Model B switched to a Hercules IXB four-cylinder engine. A later Model D was the same, except for a cast-iron grille. Leader tractors were marketed through automobile dealerships.

In 1949, as traditional tractor makers came up to speed following the lifting of World War II manufacturing restrictions, Leader Tractor went bankrupt.

The 2,800-pound Models A through D were noted for high horsepower in a small size. They were equipped with a three-point lift, PTO, muffler, and starter.

SPECIFICATIONS

A (Chrysler-powered)

Engine: 6-cylinder, vertical, inline, side valve

Bore and stroke: 3.13×4.38 in.

Displacement: 201 ci., gasoline fuel

Power: 21 drawbar hp, 30 belt hp; 3-plow rating

Transmission: 3f-1r

Top speed: 17.0 mph (with gov. o'ride)

Weight: 2,800 pounds

1944 Leader A

Long

Tarboro,
North Carolina

LONG
MODEL A

The Long Manufacturing Company, founded in 1941, first made tobacco-harvesting and -drying equipment. In 1948, it came out with the Long Model A tractor, a Farmall H–look-alike using a four-cylinder Continental engine of 162-cubic-inch displacement. This row crop tricycle tractor used a four-speed transmission and had adjustable rear-wheel treads, fenders, hydraulic lift, and a starter and lights. A maximum belt horsepower of 32 resulted in a three-plow rating with 14-inch plow bottoms.

As traditional tractor makers changed back to tractor production following World War II, Long ceased tractor operations until 1972, when they began to import tractors from England, Italy, Poland, and Romania, modifying them as necessary for the domestic market. The company, also known as LongAgri, became defunct in 2008.

SPECIFICATIONS
A

Engine: 4-cylinder, vertical, inline, side valve

Bore and stroke: 3.44×4.38 in.

Displacement: 162 ci., gasoline fuel

Power: 28 drawbar hp, 32 belt hp; 3-plow rating

Transmission: 4f-1r

Top speed: 13 mph

Weight: 3,618 lb.

NTTL# 410

1948 Long A

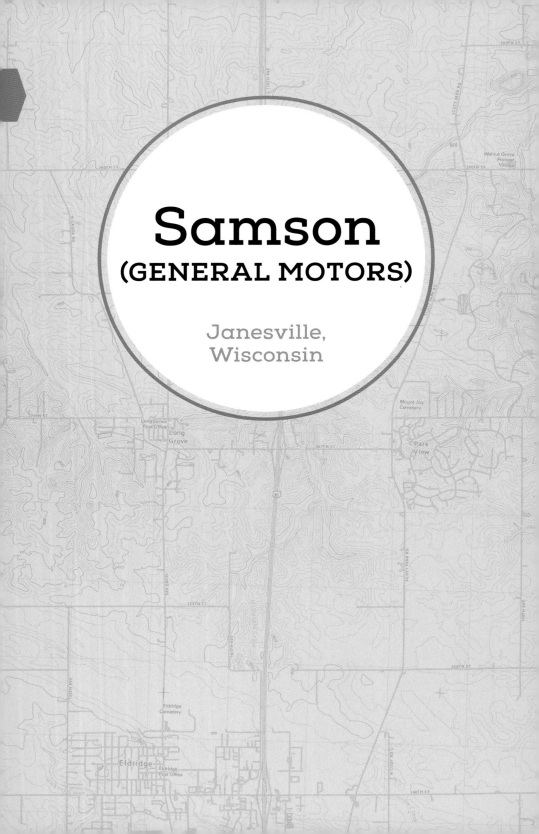

Samson
(GENERAL MOTORS)

Janesville,
Wisconsin

SAMSON
MODEL M AND
IRON HORSE

Samson Iron Works had produced a tractor called the Sieve-Grip—named for its open-faced steel wheels—beginning in 1914. It was a mildly successful seller, despite its 25-foot turning circle. In 1918, General Motors bought the outfit and moved production from Stockton, California, to Janesville, Wisconsin.

General Motors did not gain the desired foothold in the tractor business with its Sieve-Grip, mainly because of its high price, so the Model M was a completely new design, made to compete head-on with archrival Ford's Fordson tractor. The Model M looked like the Fordson but was better balanced. It had only a two-speed gearbox, while the Fordson had three speeds.

In the early 1920s, farm equipment manufacturers worked to develop a "motor cultivator," thinking that delicate crops could be cultivated by machine, rather than by hand or horse-drawn machine. General Motors Samson competed by buying the rights to an existing unit called the Jim Dandy Motor Cultivator—which they named the Iron Horse—a four-wheel-drive skid-steer unit, with belt-tightener drives for each side. The control levers were arranged so that the operator could ride and drive, or walk behind the machine and control it with reins, like a horse. Samson installed a four-cylinder Chevrolet overhead-valve engine of 171 cubic inches, providing about 10 horsepower. Top speed was 3 miles per hour.

SPECIFICATIONS

M

Engine: 4-cylinder, vertical, inline, side valve

Bore and stroke: 4.00×5.50 in.

Displacement: 276 ci., gasoline fuel

Power: 11 drawbar hp, 19 belt hp; 2-plow rating

Transmission: 2f-1r

Top speed: 3.2 mph

Weight: 3,300 lb.

NTTL# 27

1919 Samson M

R. H. Sheppard

Hanover,
Pennsylvania

SHEPPARD
MODEL SD-2, SD-3, AND SD-4

R. H. Sheppard Company was a pioneer in diesel farm tractors in the 1950s, building three sizes: the SD-2 (two-cylinder, two-plow rating), SD-3 (three-cylinder, three-plow rating), and SD-4 (four-cylinder, four-plow rating). Orchard and industrial versions of all three sizes were made. Adjustable wide fronts or dual-tricycle fronts were optional.

The most popular, the SD-3, introduced in 1949, had 4×5-inch cylinders for 189-cubic-inch displacement and weighed about 4,200 pounds. Electric starting was provided. A four-speed transmission was used with a high-low auxiliary. Hydraulics was an option. Top speed with the two-speed auxiliary was about 17 mph.

The SD-4 model, introduced in 1954, had an in-house–designed power steering unit. The unit was later applied to heavy-duty trucks and eventually became the primary product of the company. In 1957, Sheppard exited the tractor market to concentrate on marketing power steering units.

1949 Sheppard SD-2

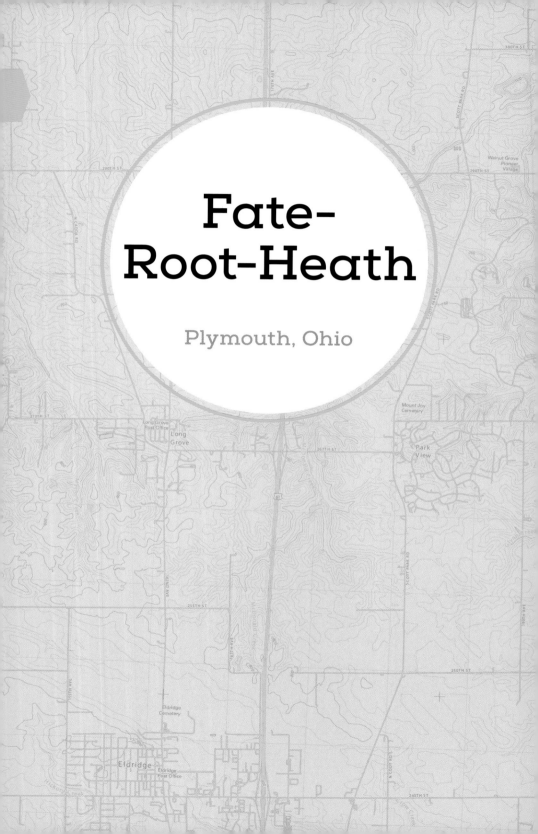

Fate-Root-Heath

Plymouth, Ohio

1936 Fate-Root-Heath Silver King

FATE-ROOT-HEATH
SILVER KING

The Fate-Root-Heath Company of Plymouth, Ohio, began building the Plymouth 10-20 tractor in 1933, renaming it the Silver King in 1935 to avoid conflict with Chrysler's Plymouth automobile. There were two versions of the Silver King, a standard tread and a tricycle with a single front wheel. A Hercules IXA engine was used in both, but this was soon changed to an IXB engine, with the bore increased from a 3- to 3.25-inch diameter. A four-speed transmission gave a normal top speed of 15 miles per hour, although with governor override, 25 miles per hour was possible.

SPECIFICATIONS
Silver King

Engine: 4-cylinder, vertical, inline, side valve

Bore and stroke: 3.25×4.00 in.

Displacement: 132.7 ci., gasoline fuel

Power: 12 drawbar hp, 20 belt hp; 2-plow rating

Transmission: 4f-1r

Top speed: 25 mph (with gov. o'ride)

Weight: 2,200 lb.

NTTL# 250

International Makes

International tractors often parallel those of US manufacturers of the same time period. Data on these tractors is not nearly as readily available as for US brands, because most American tractors are tested at the University of Nebraska, and test data is readily available.

Deutz-Fahr

Cologne,
Germany

1950 Deutz-Fahr F2L 514/50

MODELS F2L, F3M, AND F3L

Deutz, a pioneer in diesel tractors, can trace its history to Nikolaus Otto and Gottlieb Daimler, inventers of the internal combustion engine. Agricultural machinery production began in 1907. Specializing in air-cooled diesels, Deutz produced tractors that became popular in Germany after World War II. Deutz merged with Fahr, a farm implement manufacturer, in 1969, and Deutz-Fahr was taken over by SAME (Societa Anonima Motori Endothermic) in 1995.

The Deutz-Fahr F2L 514/50 tractor (introduced in 1950) used a two-cylinder

air-cooled diesel. The F3M 417 (1951) used a three-cylinder water-cooled diesel, while the F3L 514 (1953) was powered by a three-cylinder air-cooled diesel. The two-cylinder engine was started electrically, while the three-cylinder types were started by compressed air. Deutz tractors, like most European tractors, had relatively high top speeds and were generally equipped with front suspension systems to improve transport speed ride comfort.

Fendt

Marktoberdorf,
Germany

FENDT
MODEL DIESELROSS F-12

In a blacksmith shop in Marktoberdorf, Bavaria, Germany, Hermann Fendt assembled his first farm tractor in 1928. The company he founded, Fendt, prospered in the prewar years, becoming a prominent brand in Germany that specialized in Dieselross (diesel horse) tractors. Fendt used engines from Deutz, MWM (Motoren-Werke-Mannheim), and MAN (Maschinenfabrik-Augsburg-Nürnberg). In 1997, Fendt became part of AGCO (the Allis-Gleaner Corporation).

The F-12 Dieselross, built in 1957 and 1958, used a 55.2-cubic-inch single-cylinder direct injection diesel engine. It was air-cooled, had a bore and stroke of 3.86×4.72 inches, and produced 12 horsepower. Electric starting was used. The transmission had six forward speeds and two in reverse. Top speed was 12.4 miles per hour. The F-12 weighed 2,536 pounds. The F-15 was much the same, but the engine produced 15 horsepower.

1958 Fendt Dieselross F-12

Hanomag

Hannover, Germany

1939 Hanomag RL20

MODELS RL20 AND R16

Hanomag (Hannoversche Maschinenbau AG) was another old-line German manufacturing company, dating back to 1835. It first concentrated on heavy projects such as locomotives and ships. The year 1912 saw Hanomag's first efforts in the agricultural market, with the Hanomag Motor Plough. The company claims the application of diesel engines as early as 1930, and in 1957, it offered turbocharged versions. After producing a quarter-million tractors, Hanomag dropped the business in 1971. Kubota, of Japan, acquired Hanomag in 1989.

The Hanomag RL20 came out in the late 1930s and was like the Minneapolis-Moline UDLX: a field vehicle that could be driven to town. The RL20, unlike the UDLX, had a front suspension and hydraulic brakes. It was powered by a 20-horsepower four-cylinder engine and used a five forward speeds, one reverse transmission.

By the 1950s, the smaller Hanomag tractors were powered by two-cylinder four-cycle diesels. The R16 model, for example, used a 16-horsepower version of that engine.

Landini

Fabbrico, Italy

LANDINI
MODELS L25
AND DT

Landini is the oldest tractor manufacturer in Italy, with its name dating back to 1884 and tractor manufacture to 1925. The first was a hot-bulb semi-diesel of 30 horsepower, a forerunner of models with names like Velite, Buffalo, and Super. The company continued with these single-cylinder semi-diesels until 1957. The engine type was popular all over Europe, as it could run on most anything combustible, from vegetable oil to used engine oil. In 1960, Landini joined the Canadian Massey Ferguson group, which also included Perkins Engines.

Following World War II, Landini came out with the Model L25, a 262.3-cubic-inch

semi-diesel that produced 25 horsepower and used a transmission of three forward speeds and one reverse. By 1958, Landini had switched to regular diesel engines, in the form of three- and four-cylinder Perkins engines made under license. The 1958 Landini Lindinetta DT, with a 166-cubic-inch Perkins three-cylinder engine of 25 horsepower, was the first result. A six-forward-speed, two-reverse-speed transmission was provided. The DT weighed just under 5,000 pounds.

1954 Landini L25

Lanz

Mannheim, Germany

LANZ
MODELS 7506 BULLDOG AND HR9 EIL BULLDOG

Lanz started with steam engines before converting to internal combustion tractors in 1921. Their first offering was the Bulldog, production of which continued for the next thirty years. It used single-cylinder hot-bulb semi-diesel engines of 38 to 862 cubic inches displacement. The semi-diesel relied on heat, not compression, for ignition. Bulldogs were made in a variety of configurations, including crawlers. They were popular in Germany but were also made in Austria, Spain, Poland, and France. In 1955, Deere & Company acquired Lanz, and by 1970, the Lanz name had disappeared.

The Model 7506 Bulldog (1936–1952) was rated at 25 horsepower from its 287-cubic-inch one-cylinder two-cycle liquid-cooled

engine. It featured an electrical system, fender passenger seat, leaf spring front suspension, and rubber tires. A transmission of six forward speeds and one reverse was provided.

The 1939 Lanz Model HR9 Eil Bulldog ("eil" translates to "speedy") had a comfortable bench seat, full windshield, and four-wheel brakes. It also had a front suspension with a split front axle anchored in the middle and a transverse leaf spring. The single-cylinder hot-bulb two-cycle semi-diesel was of a 629-cubic-inch displacement. A six-speed shift-on-the-fly transmission gave 25 miles per hour. The cylindrical tank behind the seat held the fuel, which could be virtually any combustible liquid.

1948 Lanz Bulldog 7506

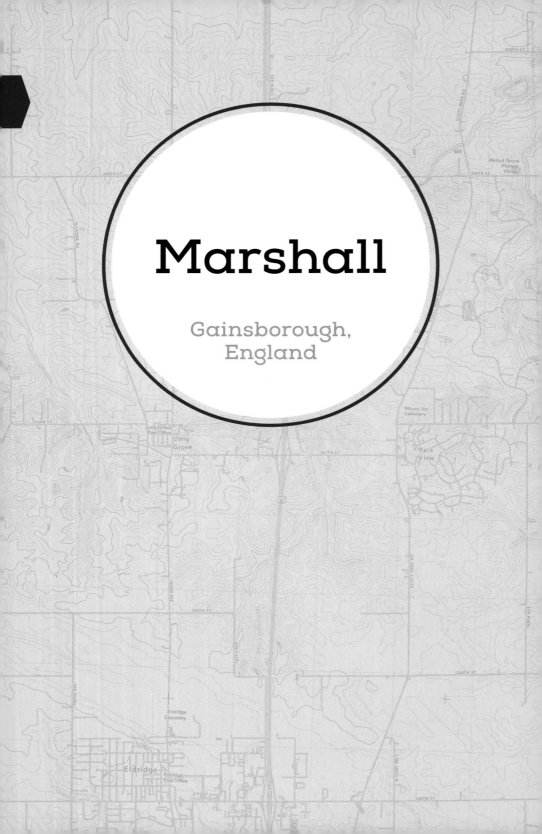

Marshall

Gainsborough,
England

MARSHALL
SERIES I
THROUGH III
AND IIIA

Marshall began with steam engines and switched to internal combustion tractors in 1908. The first of the traditional one-cylinder Marshalls was introduced in 1930. The great Field Marshall line emerged after World War II. Also at that time, Marshall merged with John Fowler & Company of Leeds, England, a maker of crawler tractors. The company went out of business in the 1970s.

Both the Field Marshall and Fowler crawlers were powered by a 310-cubic-inch single-cylinder, two-cycle diesel engine of about 40 horsepower. The wheeled Field Marshalls came in four series: Series I, II, and III had 3f/1r transmissions; the later Series III and IIIA tractors had a 6f/2r gearbox, which gave a 12 miles per hour top speed.

Starting the Field Marshall diesel required the use of a lighted wick, inserted into the cylinder head. A decompression valve was then activated, and the flywheel turned by hand. When the engine "fired," the decompression valve closed automatically. A cartridge starter was also available, but it was expensive to use and caused carbonization of the decompression valve. The latest Field Marshalls had an electric starting option.

Marshall Field Marshall Series IIIA

Porsche

Friedrichshafen,
Germany

PORSCHE
JUNIOR AND
SUPER

Dr. Ferdinand Porsche, German master automobile designer and manufacturer, also ventured into the tractor business. Flush with the success of his prewar Volkswagen "People's Car," he designed a Volksschlepper "People's Tractor." Because of the war, the concept never got past the prototype stage. In 1945, however, Dr. Porsche revived the tractor idea in the form of a two-cylinder air-cooled diesel machine.

But in 1949, tractors no longer fit in with sports cars, so the Allgaier firm, a small German tractor maker, adopted production of the Porsche tractor line. This arrangement continued through 1957, when the Mannesmann Group acquired the Porsche tractor license. Under Mannesmann, the line covered a power range from 14 to 50 horsepower. In 1964, Renault of France took over the Mannesmann Group, and the Porsche name was discontinued from tractors.

The Porsche Junior K (1949) was an 11-horsepower tractor with a 6f/2r transmission. It offered a PTO and a hydraulic implement lift. The one-cylinder air-cooled diesel displaced 50.2 cubic inches. Top speed was 13 miles per hour. The tractor (NTTL# 699) weighed about 2,600 pounds.

The Porsche Super (1959) featured a three-cylinder air-cooled diesel engine of 160.6 cubic inches, producing 37 horsepower at the PTO. An 8f/2r gearbox was provided, giving a top speed of 12 miles per hour. The Super (NTTL# 728) weighed in at 4,800 pounds.

1957 Porsche 122

Steyr

LANDMASCHINENTECHNIK

Steyr, Austria

1954 Steyr 180 Diesel

MODEL 180

Steyr was part of the Steyr-Daimler-Puch conglomerate from 1934 until 1990 and was purchased by the Case Corporation in 1996. Case IH and New Holland merged in 1999 to form CNH Global, and finally, under the giant Italian conglomerate Fiat, they formed CNH Industrial in 2013. Steyr exists today as a marque of that company. Steyr's tractors are produced in Austria and exported to Germany, Switzerland, Italy, Belgium, the Netherlands, and Luxembourg. Nineteen different tractor models are currently offered.

The Steyr 180 was manufactured from 1947 to 1954. It used a two-cylinder water-cooled 162.3-cubic-inch diesel engine, producing 26 horsepower. The transmission featured five speeds forward and one in reverse.

PHOTOGRAPHY CREDITS

Ralph W. Sanders: pp. 2–3, 6, 8–9, 11, 13, 14, 15, 16, 17, 19 (top), 21, 22, 23, 24, 29, 33, 34, 35, 36, 37, 38, 43, 45, 46, 47, 48, 49, 50, 52, 54, 56, 57, 59, 63 (below), 64 (right), 67, 69, 70, 72, 76 (above), 77, 79, 89, 90, 92 (both), 93, 95, 96–97, 98, 99 (top left), 101 (top), 104, 106, 107, 108, 109, 111 (above), 113, 117, 121, 123, 124, 125, 131, 133, 135 (top), 137, 140–141, 147, 149, 159, 160, 134, 171, 173, 175, 177, 179, 181, 183, 185, 186–187, 189, 191, 197, 199, 201

Gary A. Nelson: pp. 19 (above), 39, 40, 44, 53, 63 (left), 68, 99 (bottom left), 101 (above), 116, 118, 119, 122, 128, 136, 138–139, 145, 161, 163, 167, 169

Andrew Morland: pp. 12, 18, 20, 27, 28, 30, 31, 41, 51 (both), 58, 60, 61, 64 (top), 71, 73, 74, 75, 76 (top), 80, 81, 82, 83, 85, 87 (both), 91, 94, 102–103, 111 (top), 114, 115, 120, 126, 127, 129, 132, 135 (above), 143, 144, 146, 148, 150, 152, 153, 154–155, 156–157, 165–166, 193, 195, 203

Tharran Gaines: p. 25

INDEX

ABOUT THE AUTHOR

Robert N. Pripps has authored or co-authored dozens of
farm tractor books, including *The Tractor Factor*, *Classic
Farm Tractors*, *Vintage Ford Tractors*, *Big Book of Caterpillar*,
Big Book of Massey, and more. Pripps lives near Park Falls,
Wisconsin, where he owns a maple syrup farm.